Michael Jackson's Pocket Bar Book

Mitchell Beazley

Michael Jackson is the author of *The English Pu*
[published by Harper and Row, 1976] and the autho
ritative *World Guide to Beer* [published in 1977 b
Mitchell Beazley in the UK and Ballantine in th
USA]. He is a regular broadcaster for the BBC, an
a contributor to the Food and Drink pages of th
London *Evening Standard*. He has written countles
magazine and newspaper articles for publications a
diverse as the *New Statesman*, London, the Dubli
Evening Herald and Hugh Heffner's *Oui* magazin
published in Chicago and Los Angeles.

Michael Jackson has worked as an editor an
investigative reporter for David Frost in both
London and New York. He has travelled extensively
in Europe, India, Africa and the United States. I
1978 he was awarded the Silver medal of th
Gastronomic Academy of Germany for his contri
bution to the literature of drink. He is a consultan
to a firm of brewers in Finland, and is setting up a
International Drinks Museum for a Japanes
whisky company.

© 1979 Mitchell Beazley Publishers Limited
Text © Michael Jackson
First edition published 1979
All rights reserved.
ISBN 0 85533 200 X
Mitchell Beazley Publishers Limited
Mill House, 87–89 Shaftesbury Avenue, London W1V 7AD

Art Editor Rozelle Bentheim
Illustrations and maps Judith Dobie

Typeset by Key Film (Trendbourne) Ltd, London
Printed in England by Jolly & Barber Ltd, Rugby

Contents

Guide to symbols

(g) A generic term
(p) A proprietary brand
● Essential to a well-stocked bar
★ Standard cocktails
♥ Sweet drinks
Υ Short drinks
▌ Long drinks

Acknowledgements

I was born with a distant drop of Baltic vodka in my veins, misspent my youth in Scotland with the Singles, and married maltily into Ireland, but it was in New York some years ago that I was first persuaded to take my well-travelled typewriter to these particular pleasures. Thank you, Hugh van Dusen, for that good thought.

Through the good offices of the *Scientific American*, I was introduced to the microbiologist Professor Anthony Rose, whose work *Alcoholic Beverages* (Academic Press) has been a constant comfort to me. I have been assisted on numerous occasions over the years by Wallace Milroy, of the Soho Wine Market, and in my researches for the A-to-Z section of this book I was greatly aided by the management and staff of Del Monico's, Old Compton Street, London.

Countless barmen have helped me, often without knowing they were doing so. They just thought I wanted a drink. My special thanks to Dick, formerly of the Boomerang, Amsterdam; Domingo, of Los Fariones, Lanzarote, Canary Islands; Harry, of the Park Lane Hotel, London; Tony, of the Gloucester Hotel, London; "Hoss", of the Ute City Bank, Aspen; Victor, of Ginsberg's, San Francisco; and Armando, of the Library at the Beverly Hilton. In the matter of glassware and equipment, I have received help from many sources, including Liberty and Finch's Wine Bar.

I have further been assisted in my researches by Susan van Tijn, in Toronto; Jack Smith, in New York; Jeanette Dranoff, in Miami; and John Brooke-Smith, in London. My thanks also to George Glaze for his help with the maps in the travel and drink section.

A book as wide-ranging as this is inevitably indebted to the great writers on different areas of drink. For me, the masters are Hugh Johnson, Cyril Ray, Harry Craddock, David Embury, Trader Vic, John Doxat, Peter Hallgarten, Harriet Lembeck, the late Harold Grossman, and R.J.S. McDowall. Recommended reading is detailed on page 144.   – MJ

4

Introduction

Some people stick to one drink for life. That is not so much monogamy as masochism. A palate thus created will probably be driven to drink, and not for the taste of it.

A properly functioning palate does not work part-time. Anyone who appreciates a fine claret also cares about what came before and what is to follow. There is a place for champagne at breakfast, and an occasion for a mid-morning Gin Fizz. There is a time for a blushing apéritif or a coffee with calvados, a place for a Mint Julep and a moment for a Martini.

Which, where and when? These questions elicit here a pocketful of information, and an idea or two, in a concise form for easy reference. Whence came the great drinks, and to what ingredients and patient procedures does each owe its unique character? How are they served to best advantage? Will they marry happily, and should they be stirred or shaken?

Fashions in mixed drinks change, and the cocktail revival of the late 1970s has introduced new modes. Tequila and pisco brandy, amaretto and Galliano are just four drinks which have claimed a greater space behind the cocktail bar in the last decade. No doubt they will establish themselves in yet more mixed drinks as time goes by. There are already more mixed drinks than can ever be digested, but a selection of around 250 allows for most occasions and a great many constituents.

Those ingredients include patent apéritifs, vermouths, wines fortified and otherwise, spirits, liqueurs or cordials, and even beers. Not only are the major types and styles detailed in the *Pocket Bar Book*, but also a good many lesser-known examples to tickle the palate or the imagination.

Such information is as important to the bartender as the hardware discussed within. It is presented here in a compendium that is designed to be durable and handy. Just as the palate may be on intimate terms with Scotland and Kentucky, London and St Louis, so the drinker travels, too. A bibulous *Baedeker* should make for yet more enlightened wanderings. Such peregrinations can span a continent, they can be carried out in just one well-stocked bar, or in a cosmopolitan cocktail cabinet.

To investigate as an informed explorer is to drink for palate and pleasure. For, in the end, there are only two kinds of drinker: the discriminating and the indiscriminate.

Travel and drink

Drink has enjoyed a long and happy marriage with travel since the days when pilgrims broke their foot-sore journeys at abbeys for refreshment, sowing the seeds for Trappist beer, Bénédictine, Chartreuse and many other monastic delights. Had it not been for that early tourist Marco Polo, and the spicy souvenirs he brought home, Italian apéritifs would have a less interesting flavour. If Christopher Columbus had not made his business trip to the West Indies, taking sugar cane with him, the Caribbean would not be famous for rum.

Travel is not for feet, or bottoms strapped into the aeroplane seat; it is for the eyes, the mind, and most of all for the palate.

It is a two-way traffic, of course. The Londoner visiting Paris and ordering a Pernod may find *le scotch* being urged upon him as the height of chic. The American, carefully Gucci-shod and seeking the authentic grappa in Rome, may be smilingly offered Jack Daniel's or even Coca Cola by someone wearing sneakers. To accept would be worse than staying at home.

Nor has a country been properly visited unless a bottle or two is brought home. It may turn out to be available at the liquor store round the corner, but only the brandy which was actually bought in Spain will evoke the dust of a bullring; only the akvavit procured in Denmark will properly accompany a snack of marinaded herrings. The more authentic the drink, the more obscure and elusive it may prove to be, but half the fun lies in the chase, and the other half in the acquisition of the taste for the stuff.

The pleasures of life were never intended to be obtained easily, and it is always necessary to know the rules of the game, even in your own country. These rules may vary, too, within a single country, and invariably do so between the cosmopolitan cities and the industrial or rural regions. Both the American continent and Europe divide laterally in their drinking styles, though the change is made clearer by the Mexican frontier than by the Rhine.

In each continent, it is the northern countries where restrictions are to be found, with the inevitable reprisal of determined and often furtive drinking. It is a matter not only of religious influence, Protestant as against Catholic, but also of climate and meal-times.

Though the situation is similar in both continents, it is more starkly evident in Europe. Iceland is officially dry except for near-beer, and there are severe restrictions on the sale of alcohol in Norway, Sweden and Finland (but not in Denmark).

The northern European scurries home from work for dinner, sometimes as early as 6.00, and will be persuaded back out into the cold night only for a serious drinking engagement. The southerner, perhaps having had a midday siesta, works later, then dallies for apéritifs before rounding off the day with dinner at 9.00 or 10.00, washed down with wine, followed by digestifs, and perhaps taken outdoors in a balmy evening. The northerner is the single-minded drinker, but the relaxed southerner actually consumes more alcohol in the course of his protracted dining. Even in northern countries like The Netherlands and Germany, it is the Catholic southern provinces which have the bacchanalian pre-Lenten carnivals.

Islamic states can take a rather spoilsport view of alcohol, though those with a colonial hangover or an important tourist trade may be more pragmatic. In the Orient, Japan has not only become a major whisky-drinking nation but also an important brewing country. Australia, founded on rum, and now a wine-growing nation, is well known to have an insatiable thirst for beer. This was fostered by early-closing regulations, happily now lifted.

The Americas

North America – It is a paradox that North America has probably the highest standard of bartending in the world yet the most tangled web of restrictions upon the serving of alcohol.

The skill of American bartenders may be taken for granted in the United States and Canada, but the ability to produce such a wide range of mixed drinks on request is in many other countries the sole preserve of the grand hotel. Other countries may have their gin-and-tonics, even their Dry Martinis, though less often, but the Manhattan and Old Fashioned, the Screwdriver and Harvey Wallbanger are the American way of drinking and no one else's.

Yet, for all its artistry in the business of serving alcohol, North America has failed to contrive a place for sociable drinking which is as consistent, as readily recognizable, or as much a part of the national culture as the English pub or continental European café. Many an American bar is as much a restaurant, a condition that the law encourages, and those intended exclusively for serious drinkers seem to be darkened even today by the still looming shadow of Prohibition.

Within a state, counties may exercise their option to impose local restrictions to bizarre effect. Over the years, some have forbidden women from venturing near the bar counter; others have insisted that any pre-dinner drinks must be drained before an order can be taken for wine.

In many parts of the United States, and in Canada, liquor stores are a state monopoly, and are often drab and uninviting places. Canada has its

The Americas

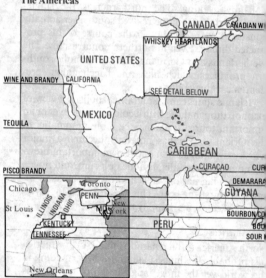

own local option system, and the province of Saskatchewan is notably unfriendly towards the drinker. In Quebec and Alberta, taverns and beverage rooms have a tradition of sexist behaviour.
Mexico – There are two distinct locations for everyday drinking in Mexico. The *cantina* is for men only; the *bar* for ladies as well. Both types of establishments open at midday and do not close until midnight or 1.00 in the morning. Cabaret bars stay open until 3.00 or 4.00 in the morning. Drinking is usually accompanied by snacks, known as *botanas*, such as tacos, tortillas or pork chops. Dinner is not eaten until 9.00 or later.

The enthusiasm of the Mexicans for hard liquor is such that their Government runs advertising campaigns to try and wean them off tequila, mezcal and even pulque, and on to beer, "the drink of moderation". The determined drinkers respond by submerging a glass of tequila in their beer. This is called a *submarino*. Or there is a 4-to-1 combination of pulque and beer known as a *calichal*.

The tequila-style ritual of lime and salt is sometimes applied to beers, which include not only conventional Pilsener-style brews but also lagers of the amber Vienna mode (as exemplified by the popular Dos Equis brand), Müncheners (like Leon Negra) and seasonal specials (such as Nochebuena).

The Caribbean – The lands of late-night drinking, at "cold supper shops". Customs vary from island to island, but favourite supper snacks include a herby soup called *callaloo*, salted and pickled fish and pork dishes in pepper sauces, with a variety of relishes, corn meal dishes, *bammie* cassava bread, and confections of green banana or plantain.

The drink is rum, of course, with a variety of local punches. Don't forget that the Caribbean provided the world's cocktail bars with such interestingly diverse ingredients as curaçao, Angostura, orgeat and falernum.

South America – Drinking modes vary from that of the basic *cantina* to the stylish café life of some big cities. Socially aspirant South Americans insist upon scotch, often quite ersatz, but the subcontinent provides an abundance of alcoholic exotica for the adventurous and brave visitor.

This varies from the very occasional tequila-type spirit in the far north through Indian distillates of corn to the less intimidating vermouths of Argentina. Such distractions aside, the true national spirits are always forms of either rum or brandy: anis-flavoured rums in Colombia and Ecuador; pisco brandy in Peru, Chile and Bolivia; a famous rum variation called cachaca (or caxaca) in Brazil; another called caña in Uruguay and Argentina. In wine-growing countries such as Uruguay and Argentina, grappa is also sometimes to be found.

Predictably, coffee and chocolate are popular drinks in certain countries, often with a spirit accompaniment. In the Hispanic tradition, snacks are often served with drink. In Argentina, the flavour of drinking snacks becomes Italian, with splendid meaty sandwiches and iced confections.

The British Isles

The visitor to Britain is customarily puzzled by the idiosyncratic drinking hours, the uncold beer, and the frequent lack of food in pubs.

Though drinking hours vary depending upon the

local authority, they always ensure two or three dry hours in the afternoon. In the cities, hours are commonly 11.00 in the morning until 3.00 in the afternoon, then 5.30 until 11.00 in the evening. Country times are usually half an hour earlier all round.

In parts of Wales, pubs are closed on Sundays, to the delight of private clubs. Scotland has, sometimes within a single municipality, a confusing mixture of extreme restrictions in some places and all-day opening in others. In Ireland, on both sides of the border, bars open from 10.00 in the morning until 11.00 or 11.30 in the evening, usually closing for just one hour in mid-afternoon so that the priest may take a drink in peace.

Uncold beer is another matter – it is, in fact, essential that both English ales and Irish stouts are

The British Isles

served at a natural cellar temperature; further chilling ruins the flavour of top-fermented beers.

The pub is a place for drinking and talking. If it is a community's local, it is a social centre, not a dining room. Though some pubs serve excellent snacks, or even sit-down meals, others defend themselves against the would-be diner by offering him a wrapped pork-pie, a stale sandwich, or even less.

The Nordic countries – The drinkers of Iceland, Norway, Sweden and Finland are most resilient and inventive in the face of state restrictions on the production and supply of alcohol. They manage to consume a greater volume of spirits per head than their libertarian but beery neighbours the Danes.

Each of these five countries produces a similar style of spirits, described in a variety of spellings by the synonymous generic terms aquavit and brännvin. Finland, historically linked with Russia, also uses the term vodka.

By whichever name, these drinks are variously distilled from grain or potatoes, and everywhere produced both in neutral and flavoured versions. Caraway, dill, arrowroot and a wide variety of interesting plants are used as flavourings, and berry fruits are also very popular, especially in Finland.

The Finns make a wide variety of liqueurs from unusual fruits such as the cloudberry and Arctic bramble, and three or four sparkling wines from the whitecurrant. This latter notable category includes one brand, Cavalierii, which is made by the champagne method.

In Denmark, a family recipe for cherry liqueur has made the Heering family famous for more than 150 years. The seafaring Danes use madeira to flavour one aquavit, and the Swedes acquired a taste for Japanese arrak on their travels.

The Finns were among Europe's first brewers, and beer remains popular in this part of the world. Norway has a pure-beer law, although its many home-brewers have been known to flavour their products with juniper and sappy alder twigs. A similar brew, called sahti, is made in Finland, often in the sauna.

The Netherlands – The Dutch "brown café", wood-panelled and smoke-stained, is a first cousin of the English pub, though it opens for longer hours. Some cafés serve lunch, and remain open until 1.00 in the morning. Others don't open until 6.00 in the evening, and close at 3.00 in the morning.

Dutch lunch is often a sandwich or snack, The visitor may enjoy a salted herring eaten at a street stall, followed by a visit to a café for a brimming glass of jenever gin and a few beers. For the Dutchman, a "happy hour" jenever or two on the way home precedes an early dinner, though the drinker who dallies can usually find a snack in the café, such as various types of sausage or meatball.

In addition to jenever, Dutch cafés serve a variety

of colourful liqueurs and ersatz brandies, and regional specialities like beerenburg bitters, from Friesland. Amsterdam has three well-known "tasting-rooms"—bars specializing in liqueurs and traditional Dutch mixed drinks. These are Wynand Fockinck, in Pijlsteeg; Drie Flesches, Gravenstraat; and Admiraal, Herengracht.

The biggest jenever distillery is near Amsterdam, though the drink was invented in Leiden and is historically associated with the town of Schiedam.

Belgium – The town of Hasselt, in the province of Limburg, is Belgium's best-known centre for the production of jenever gin, though the past importance of Ghent has left that city with a particularly keen taste for the spirit, and several other places have their own local liqueurs.

During the period when the Americans were introducing Prohibition and the British their curious

Northern Europe

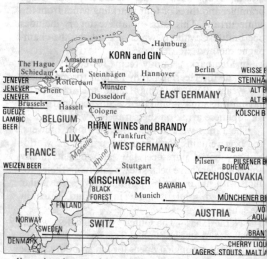

licensing laws, with temperance movements active in many countries, Belgium imposed a bizarre range of legislation to restrict the sale of spirits. Although this is now frequently ignored, it remains extant. One paradoxical law, originally intended to prevent the poor from buying spirits, insists that the purchaser in a liquor store must take at least two litres.

Another astonishing measure forbids altogether the sale of spirit in cafés, thus encouraging a Belgian taste for extremely strong beers. These include "scotch ales" and top-fermented Trappist brews of around 10%. Most Belgian towns have their own speciality beers, and Brussels is especially noted for its gueuzelambic variations, including a cherry brew called kriek. The Belgians prove in some years to be the world's heaviest drinkers of beer per capita, and always rank in this respect alongside Germany and Czechoslovakia.

Cafés may open when they wish, and their habits are most erratic. Many of them serve no food, since Gallic influence decrees that eating is too serious a matter for casual surroundings.

Germany – What the rest of the world identifies as the schnapps of Germany is the clear grain spirit usually known locally as korn, and often washed down with a chaser of beer. This drink, and the closely related Steinhäger gin, are especially popular in the north.

In the Rhine and other wine regions, the grape provides an occasion for numerous local festivals throughout the summer and autumn. German wines and brandies are drunk on their own, and the latter with coffee, but they are more commonly served during and after meals.

Kirschwasser and related brandies such as enzian are popular in the German-speaking parts of France and Switzerland as well as Baden-Württemberg and Bavaria. The Germans particularly prize kirschwasser from the Black Forest.

For all their variety of drinks, the Germans regard beer without question as the national tipple. The Bavarians have by far the most breweries, drink beer with their mid-morning snack, retain the litre stein for their autumn festivals, and have sufficiently warm weather to take their Maytime bock at leisure in beer-gardens. These are sometimes described as beer cellars, but that is merely a reference to the place where the casks are kept. Imitation bierkellers in other countries are really modelled on a quite different institution, the beer hall, often with brass bands and singing.

Germany uses several different names for drinking places. A gasthaus is an inn, which also serves food; a wirtschaft can be any type of drinking place; a wirtshaus means the same, but with a hint of moral censure; a pinte is a rough, simple drinking place; a kneipe is a matey drinking place, perhaps for students; a destille is, in the parlance of Berlin, a harddrinking joint. Most of these establishments open around midday and close around midnight. Those that don't serve meals may provide snacks of sausage or cheese with bread. As in Austria and northern Italy, some patisseries serve alcohol.

13

France

The country of the café. The price of your drink ascends as you move from the bar-stool to the table, to the terrace. The question is not only where to drink but also what to drink, with such an embarrassment of choice.

Vermouths and patent aperitifs are especially popular throughout France though they originate from a loosely defined area straddling the Alps. The

France

same is true of kir, a mix of white wine and black currant liqueur which originates from Burgundy. Like Pernod, pastis is a national drink, though it is particularly popular in Provence.

Wine may be drunk at any time, by the glass if so desired, but is primarily ordered with meals. A French worker may have half a litre with his lunch rounded off with coffee and calvados, the latter being an extremely popular digestif.

Of the brandies, calvados, cognac and armagnac are produced in rigidly demarcated areas, but the eaux-de-vie of Alsace are not, and they straddle the frontiers of Switzerland and Germany. The marc type of brandy is produced everywhere, but with special pride in Burgundy.

A surprisingly large amount of beer is drunk in France, especially in the summer. Most of it is of the bottom-fermented type, the best coming from Alsace, but some interesting top-fermented beers are produced in the Region du Nord.

France is very much of the southern school, with drinking usually related to eating. Depending upon the latitude, dinner may be taken between 8.30 and 10.00. Though restaurants may serve casual drinkers on the terrace, cafés rarely provide more than a toasted sandwich. Except in the big cities, they close before midnight.

Iberia

Spain – In no country does the grape display a greater virtuosity: sherry or montilla as an apéritif; wine as a casual drink or with meals, from a communal skin *bota* in the north or a glass *porrón* in Catalonia; malaga, tarragona and a considerable variety of other fortified dessert wines; brandies as digestifs or just as hard liquor.

In the bar and more especially the all-purpose café, the delight of Spanish drinking is the range of accompanying snacks, known as tapas. These vary from such simple pleasures as hard manchego cheese to toro's testicles before the bullfight for those with the *cojones* to manage either.

Most Spanish bar snacks are meals in themselves; salads made with olives, beans, chick-peas, roasted nuts and small mushrooms, in oil, vinaigrette, marinades, garlic or pepper sauces; a wide

variety of shellfish, squid and octopus, cooked in their own juices, grilled, fried or in sauces; smoked meats, piquant sausages, small birds; snails; or just wedges of the famous Spanish omelette.

The Spanish eat dinner between 9.00 and 11.00. Their two native liqueurs, Calisay and Cuarenta y Tres, are popular digestifs. In the country, cafés close between midnight and 1.00; in holiday resorts, they may remain open until 2.00 or later.

Portugal – Most port goes overseas, and the little that is left is apt to be reserved for special occasions. The affluent drink white port as an apéritif, sometimes with ice. Less fashionable apéritifs are fruit wines (*ginginha*) and "absinthe", poured over sugar through a slotted spoon.

Portugal produces a wide range of wines, among which vinhos verdes are well regarded locally. A noted moscatel is produced at Setubal.

A universally popular hard liquor and digestif is bagaçeira, the Portuguese version of marc or grappa, which is usually drunk with black coffee. There are several very local liqueurs and a rare eau-de-vie called medronho, made from arbutus berries.

Drinking snacks are not always offered. If they are, they may include pickled beans, snails, small birds, marmalade (a Portuguese invention), made from quince and perhaps served with cheese, and a wide range of pastries, notably tiny glazed custard creams.

Southern Europe

Italy – What might be called the fruit-brandy belt stretches from southern Germany into Austria, Hungary and Yugoslavia, and it has through the course of political history now provided yet more alcoholic pleasures for the already well-served drinkers of Italy.

Yugoslavia's maraschino country, Dalmatia, once belonged to the republic of Venice. In the political confusion which followed World War II, some maraschino makers hopped across the border into Italy.

At the same time, the firm of Zwack, famous for its apricot brandy, followed the trade routes of the old Austro-Hungarian empire from Budapest to Vienna and Genoa. The Hungarians still make apricot brandy, with fruit from the Kecskemét region, while Zwack retain the trademark Barack Palinka for theirs. Zwack also make their famous Unicum bitters in Genoa, in Italy's heartland of herbal specialities and vermouths.

At its borders with Austria and Switzerland, Italy can be a surprisingly cold and northern country. Some bars there open at 6.00 or 7.00 in the morning to provide outdoor workers with grappa and coffee to start the day. Still more than the endless aperitifs and digestifs, coffee is the ubiquitous drink of Italy; it even goes into sambuca.

Another sign of past Austrian influence in the northern cities is the fancy patisserie, which also

serves ice-creams, coffee, late afternoon apéritifs. It
s the custom in these establishments to order from
he cashier, pay, obtain a receipt and pass that to the
waiter so that he knows what to bring. The patisserie closes early in the evening, but ordinary cafés
and bars stay open to 11.00, midnight or later.

A particularly Italian institution is the mescita, a
wine shop that sells the grape by the glass, or by
he bottle to take away. Although only chianti and
the Sicilian marsala have a popular worldwide
reputation, Italy produces more wine than France.

There is much more for the bibber to enjoy
before, during and after the interminable lunches
and equally gargantuan dinners, starting around
8.00 in the north and 9.30 or 10.00 in the south.

Southern Europe

Greece – The Greeks do not drink heavily, nor do
they like to take alcohol without food. The Greek
equivalent to the pub or café is the kafenion, a male
haunt for late afternoon and early evening, for talk
and backgammon, ouzo with snacks of cheese and
olives, or coffee with honey pastries.

Ouzo, known in some places as douzico and
others as raki, is both a casual drink and an apéritif.
It is diluted with water, which is provided on all
occasions. A glass of water and some fruit or jam
are often provided as a gesture of hospitality, and
should never be left untouched.

Retsina and a wide variety of other Greek wines
go with dinner in the taverna, starting at 8.30 or
9.00 and lasting well into the small hours, with
digestifs of mastika or local orange liqueurs.

Anyone can mix a drink for a friend or two. To serve apéritifs for a dozen dinner guests, or cocktails for 50 people at a party, takes a little more organization. The coward's way out is to hire a bartender but, as always in life, bravery is more fulfilling. Surely the host who enjoys an interesting drink will want to provide a personal touch for the guests?

How, though, to mix the Martinis while stirring a little conversation? It must all happen in the same room, with no dashing back and forth to the kitchen while yet more thirsty guests arrive. Whatever the protestations of the cramped Manhattan apartment-dweller or the determinedly unvulgar English party-giver there is something to be said for having a bar in the home.

It needn't be a shrine for conspicuous consumption, a pocket Ritz, or a monument to bad taste. It may simply be a cocktail cabinet that has fold-out working surfaces, some Deco delight fit for Noël Coward's *Design for Living*; a sturdy trolley with a shelf or two; or a wall unit with a handy recess for a refrigerator.

The need for ice, and plenty of it, not to mention a roomy, sturdy, hard-wearing working surface, and a double sink for washing and rinsing, all argue the case for a purpose-built bar, even if its utilitarian quality is masked in a tireless extravaganza of pine, bamboo, plush or ostrich feathers.

Vermouths and patent apéritifs taste better if they are kept lightly chilled; white wines should obviously be kept cold, as should dry sherries; but only aquavits and Slavic vodkas intended to be drunk straight require intense refrigeration. If cocktail glasses are kept in the refrigerator, they will present a stylish frostiness when filled.

A shelf under the counter, but not too low, can also accommodate the most frequently used base spirits, a bottle each of dry and sweet vermouth, bitters, soda, and sizable jugs of fruit juices. Replacements can be kept behind the bars, along with fancier drinks and liqueurs. This way, the bartender does not have to turn his or her back on the guests too often. For the same reason, the bar should be a simple, unfussy shape, and every drink and piece of equipment should have its regular place, to which it is returned immediately after use. It may be tedious to be so methodical, but it saves undignified scrambles on the night, as any professional bartender will testify.

lemon-squeezer or juice-extractor of one sort or nother is vital. No particular design can be elected s the best, since it is a matter of personal taste as to vhich handles most easily and extracts the juice nost efficiently, but the choice of this simple piece of quipment bears careful consideration. If there are o be many guests, squeeze plenty of juice before-and for mixed drinks, but not so far in advance hat it loses its freshness.

Ice containers come in innumerable designs, most f them aesthetically offensive. Look for capacity nd efficient insulation, and have a spare one so that uests can help themselves. If white wines or cham-agne are to be served, a bucket ice container in vhich they can be cooled will also be required.

Tongs are more efficient than a spoon when ice is o be put into a glass, and they don't carry any nwanted water.

Ice-crushers come in various designs, and one ood example is shown. Crushed ice (sometimes t is described as being shaved) is required for frappé drinks, daiquiris and a variety of other treats. Crushers can usually be adjusted to produce racked ice for drinks like the Old Fashioned. Otherwise, wrap cubes in a tea-towel and crack hem with a kitchen mallet or empty bottle. If drinks are mixed in an electric blender, whole ice ubes will damage the blades, but this problem does ot arise with mixers made especially for bars.

Jugs for iced water or fruit juice should have an nvoluted pourer to hold back the cubes. This type f jug can also be used as a mixing glass, with no eed for a strainer.

A scoop is needed to load crushed or cracked ice nto a drink, mixing glass or shaker.

The bartender's friend is an all-in-one device hat opens corked or crown-topped bottles, and ans. It is a handy back-up even if a more elaborate orkscrew is preferred and a bottle-opener per-nanently fixed to the bar.

Measures. Each side of the Atlantic has its own ariation on the fluid ounce, and on the gill, with he centilitre offering yet a fifth system of measure-nent. So long as all ingredients are measured by the ame means, it doesn't matter which of these scales s used. Since most classic cocktails originate from he Americas, the "jigger" used in bars in the United States is a common basic measurement in ecipes. A jigger contains $1\frac{1}{2}$ US ounces, and they are the unit of measurement used in *The Pocket Bar Book*. The measure usually found in British cocktail bars contains just under one US ounce, though the shortfall is hardly significant. This smaller measure contains 0.96 US fluid ounce, which

Ice tongs

Ice-crusher   *Ice scoop*   *Iced water jug*

equals 1.0 Imperial fluid ounce, or ⅕th of an Imperial gill. In pubs in the UK (though not Scotland), a still smaller measure, ⅙th of a gill, is used.

Bitters bottles are fitted with caps like those used to pour vinegar or salad oil. This means that a "dash" of Angostura or orange bitters can be shaken without the need for measurement.

Mixing glasses come in various shapes and sizes, but are always big enough for the preparation of several drinks at once. The mixing glass, sometimes known as a bar glass, is for drinks that are to be stirred, not shaken. These are drinks that are intended to be clear, not cloudy, and which would be particularly harmed by the greater dilution caused in shaking. After being stirred, the drink should be strained into a cocktail glass straight up, or on to fresh ice in a larger glass.

Muddlers also come in various sizes, large ones for use with a mixing glass and smaller ones for the drinker's own amusement. They have a bulbous end and are intended for crushing sugar and pounding mint in a drink. A similar device with a paddle-like end is called a swizzle-stick. The shaft is rubbed between the palms of the hands so that the paddle agitates the drink. This trick is intended to calm overexcited drinks and enliven flat ones, but has little useful effect in either case. Still, a swizzle-stick has harmless decorative value in a drink.

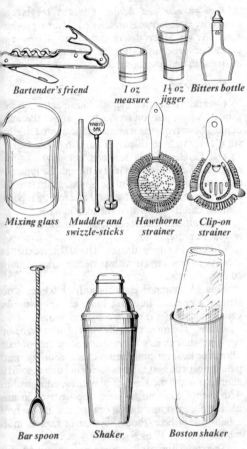

Bartender's friend *1 oz measure* *1½ oz jigger* *Bitters bottle*

Mixing glass *Muddler and swizzle-sticks* *Hawthorne strainer* *Clip-on strainer*

Bar spoon *Shaker* *Boston shaker*

Strainers. The classic strainer made by the firm of Hawthorne has its name spelled out in the holes. Another popular type clips on to the mixing glass.

A bar spoon is used to stir drinks in a mixing glass, or after they have been served. The "wrong" end can be used as a muddler.

A shaker is used in drinks that contain fruit juices, syrups, very thick liqueurs, or any ingredients that demand a thorough mix. Because the ice gets knocked about in the mixer, there may be considerable dilution, and a clear drink cannot easily be produced. A shaker of classic design incorporates a strainer in the topmost chamber. This simplifies the serving of drinks. A Boston shaker, comprising one half of metal and the other of glass, is easier to break open but less convenient in the pouring, since a separate strainer is required.

21

Paring knife and board. Easy to forget, ye obviously necessary. How else could one produc with easy efficiency slivers and twists of lemon o cucumber peel, and slices of orange, which ar crisp, clean and handsome?

Useful glasses

Cocktail. Essential, elegant, and neatly propor tioned. A stem just long enough to protect the smal conical bowl from the warmth of the hand. Opening sufficiently wide to display a garnish. Max 4 oz.

Old Fashioned. For any cocktail served on the rocks. Also doubles for whisky, though the typically chunky Old Fashioned glass is less attractive fo that purpose than the cut-crystal and faintly tapered tumbler traditionally used for scotch. 6 oz.

Highball. An intermediate size which can serve several purposes. 8 oz.

Collins. For long drinks. The taller the better Always narrow, often with perfectly straight sides 10 oz.

Sour. A stemmed glass for a drink which is no strictly a cocktail but isn't long, either. A simila glass is sometimes used for a Fizz. 5–6 oz.

Ballon. The most versatile glass of all. Ostensibl for wine, though its size emphasizes the rule of half filling (or less) for both bouquet and sobriety. Pin patent apéritifs best express their cool and colourfu character atop the stem of a well-rounded ballon with plenty of room to swish the ice around an contemplate a sunny slice of orange. It will even hol a half-pint of beer, though a straight glass is mor *macho*. Approx 10 oz.

Sherry. Those tall schooners are stilted an lumpy and do not hold the bouquet. A dry sherry ir a large glass warms before it is drunk. Better to have a small glass which can be refilled from a cooled bottle. For a fino, a delicate glass which turns in very gently to hold the bouquet. Say 2 oz.

Liqueur. Rich, sweet liqueurs are served in small quantities. 1–2 oz.

Pousse-café. A tall, narrow liqueur glass for this stripy production.

Snifter. The traditional brandy glass, well rounded to be warmed in the palm of the hand, with a short stem. The rim turns in to hold the powerful bouquet. Enormous glasses look silly.

Champagne. The traditional saucer was intended to cope with the custom of dunking madeira cake. It can also accommodate the garnish on a cham pagne cocktail better than the narrow tulip glass,

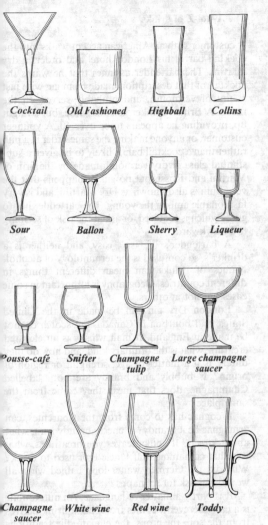

Cocktail   **Old Fashioned**   **Highball**   **Collins**

Sour   **Ballon**   **Sherry**   **Liqueur**

Pousse-café   **Snifter**   **Champagne tulip**   **Large champagne saucer**

Champagne saucer   **White wine**   **Red wine**   **Toddy**

which is preferable not only on aesthetic grounds but also because it retains the sparkle better.

White wine. A long stem so that the hand does not warm the drink. A tall, narrow bowl to retain the cold. A fine line for a delicate wine.

Red wine. Solid looking to match the fatness of a burgundy or claret, with a shortish stem and a well-rounded bowl to be embraced warmly. The rim wide enough to let the wine breathe.

Toddy. Fireproof glasses with handles are useful for hot drinks.

23

The A–to–Z of drinks

A customer with an American accent walks into the cocktail bar of his London hotel and orders a dry martini. The bartender assumes that he wants the cocktail of that description, made from gin with just a hint of vermouth, and probably served on the rocks. A British drinker gets the same, but straight up, providing he appears to be over 40. A younger customer, or anyone making the same order in a pub rather than a cocktail bar, is likely to be given a substantial glass of dry vermouth made by the firm of Martini and Rossi, but no gin. It happens that the vermouth is also known as Dry Martini, and is very fashionable among the young. The bartender has to guess which is required, or ask at the risk of seeming to be awkward.

A bartender's life isn't easy, and neither is a drinker's, so confused is the terminology of alcohol. Names of drinks can mean different things in different countries. Geography is important in some cases but not in others.

London Dry gin can be made in the United States, and bourbon in Canada, but scotch cannot be made in England. If malt whisky is an elevated creature, what is the ordinary kind, and how do they differ? Is it a matter of age, strength, or region of origin? If bubbly and brandy are both labelled Champagne, does that mean they come from the same place?

If cognac has to come from the Charentes, can armagnac be a brandy? If cherry brandy isn't, what about kirsch? If vodka leaves you breathless, what was that cinnamon stuff Uncle Igor used to drink? Why did the German waiter look baffled when all we did was ask for schnapps?

It is partly a matter of language. An automobile is a car wherever it comes from, but a drink derives from the soil, the crops, the climate, the traditions of its native land, and usually speaks a foreign language. Not only may it be unique to its home country, but it may also have a mystique. These have long been produced by Alpine monks, and latterly by Madison Avenue.

The advertisements are decent, honest and truthful, but so is Scotch mist as far as it goes. The labels are awash with information, but they tell everything and nothing.

The difficulty lies in knowing which of the words on the bottle mean what. When the protestations of antiquity and authenticity have been dealt with, it

24

emains to be made clear quite what drink the bottle contains, and whether it has to be categorized according to sweetness, dryness or style. No doubt the maker has indicated his own name, but if he happens to be a sizeable corporation, he may further add a brand-name for this particular product. For the drinker bent upon alcoholic exploration, it can all be rather confusing.

Not that things are easy for the manufacturer. Cointreau is a liqueur house, but the firm specifically applies its name to its famous brand of triple sec. If people ask for a Cointreau, they get the firm's triple sec. Why? Because after Cointreau had pioneered the product, lots of other firms produced drinks which they called triple sec. They could do this because triple sec was accepted as a generic term for a type of curaçao. Both of those terms are used in ordering, but no one ever asks for an orange liqueur, which is what they describe.

Perhaps orange liqueur is too vague a term, but drinkers do ask for "a peppermint" or usually "a crème de menthe" more often than they use brand-names like Freezomint or Pippermint Get. The situation is infinitely more complicated in the matter of patent liqueurs, of which there are thousands, the greatest number produced in southern Europe. Manufacturers emphasize their brand names, and play down generics, to protect their formulae.

There are scores of sambucas, but there is only one Galliano. There are several pastis, but there is only one Pernod. Anyone can make rock'n'rye, but there is only one Forbidden Fruit.

Some of the more commonly used terms are defined and discussed on the pages which follow. A generic term is identified by a **(g)** and a proprietary brand by a **(p)**. Since two different proof systems operate in the English-speaking world, alcoholic strength is quoted as a percentage by volume, a much more readily comprehensible measure. If the percentage of alcohol by volume is doubled, it produces the American proof figure. If it is multiplied by seven and divided by four, it produces the British proof figure. Drinks are often marketed at several strengths, and this may vary according to local laws; in some cases, the figure given is an average or an estimate, and is merely intended as a general guide.

If a drink is marked •, it should be available in a well-stocked bar.

Abricotine (p) 30–35% Sweet, apricot-flavoured after-dinner liqueur based on brandy. From the French liqueur house of Garnier. See also *Apry* and *Apricot brandy*.

Absinthe (g) 68% The Green Muse, because it inspired Hemingway and seduced the brushes of Degas, Toulouse-Lautrec and Picasso. The Green Goddess for its questionably aphrodisiac qualities. The Forbidden Elixir because it is banned in its native Switzerland, its adoptive France and, effectively, everywhere else. Its eponymous ingredient wormwood (*Artemesia absinthum*) was blamed for madness and death. The means of extraction then used, and the compounds subsequently formed, were potentially harmful only in immense excess. Absinthe was replaced by dry *Anis* drinks of around 45% typified by *Pernod*. See also *Pastis*, in which liquorice is the prominent ingredient. Both are drunk as hard liquors, especially in Provence and as apéritifs throughout France. A wide variety of similar-tasting liqueurs is made in Europe by the infusion in neutral spirits of aniseed, liquorice, fennel and other plants.

Acquavite (g) It is a measure of man's community that so many European tribes agreed at an early stage that spirits were—as acquavite translates—"the water of life". Acquavite is an Italian general term for spirits. The more common *Akvavit* and *Aquavit* spellings belong to Scandinavia. The French follow suit by calling their brandies collectively *Eaux-de-vie*, and the idea recurs in the Gaelic uisgebeatha, etymologically the parent of whisk(e)y.

Advocaat (g) 15% Dutch egg-and-brandy liqueur. Legend has it to be a misunderstood version of an equally thick avocado drink encountered by Dutch mariners in the West Indies. Others submit that it leads the drinker to talk with the eloquence of an advocate, or that it was once favoured as a tipple by lawyers. In truth, it is a talkative drink only in that it is popular with gossipy old ladies in search of an innocent and sustaining pick-me-up, with teenage girls in a lemonade concoction called a snowball, and at Dutch christenings, for which occasion it may be flavoured with cinnamon. Flavours such as mokka and chocolate are available in Germany.

Aguardiente (g) "Fire-water". Generic term in the Spanish language for spirit drinks. In Spain, it may specifically refer to a coarse, brandy-like spirit made from grape skins, stalks and pips, and comparable with French *Marc*, Italian *Grappa*, etc. In Latin America, especially Ecuador and Colombia, it can refer to a coarse sugar cane spirit often flavoured with aniseed.

Akvavit (g) 40–45% Name broadly applied to all the principal indigenous spirits of the Scandinavian countries, irrespective of the flavour (also Akvaviittee and *Aquavit*). The akavit spelling is most common in Denmark, where Aalborg is the most popular brand. A neutral spirit is produced from potatoes if they are in season, or from grain, and redistilled with flavourings, in the manner of gin. Caraway is the most popular flavour, although dill is also typical. Drink ice-cold in a small glass that has first been frosted in the refrigerator. An interesting apéritif with a chaser of beer and a marinaded herring hor d'oeuvre. See also *Acquavite*.

Ale (g) 3.0–5.5% (except for special strong brews) Top-fermented beer in the British style, although approximations exist in North America. Has a hearty smack of hops, and usually a reddish-copper colour. In Britain, preferred unpasteurized, at room temperature, by the pint. Bass, from Burton, is a classic example.

Aliziergeist (g) 45% Fruit brandy in the *Eau-de-vie* style, made in Alsace from the berries of the wild service tree.

Allasch (g) 35–40% Sickly speciality liqueur which is a version of *Kümmel* with the addition of almonds, aniseed and other flavourings. Named after a castle where the original was produced in Latvia.

Almond Several companies produce crème d'amandes (g), which is usually rather sweet. Crème de noyau (g) has an almond flavour, although it is commonly made from peach and apricot kernels. Crushed almonds are used in the production of *Amaretto* (g) along with apricots. Non-alcoholic almond syrups such as orgeat are also used in cocktails.

Alt The German word for old, specifically applied to the top-fermented, copper-coloured beers of North Rhine-Westphalia, notably produced in Düsseldorf and Münster. "Old" because top-fermentation predates the bottom-fermentation method used to produce the better-known German beers. Altbier (g) 4%+ is served in cylindrical glasses and is the basis of a spring-time fruit punch.

- **Amaretto (g)** 24–28% After-dinner liqueur with almond flavour, made in Italy from apricot kernels, and very popular in the United States. Said to have first been made in Saronno in 1525 as a tribute to artist Bernadino Luini by his model. The loving associations are underlined by a well known brand called Amaretto di Amore (p). Sometimes served super-indulgently with delicious amaretto-flavoured biscuits wrapped in tissue-paper. Useful in the cocktail bar, and occasionally in the kitchen.

Amaro (g) The Italian word for bitter. Generically used to describe the many patent bitter liqueurs produced in Italy. Amaro, usually dark brown in colour, are made from herbs, plants and tree barks. They are diluted and served with ice as apéritifs, and served neat as digestifs. There are at least 500 established brands, some containing little alcohol, others up to 45%.

Amer Picon (p) 21% Sometimes known simply as Picon (Amer is French for bitter). Patent aperitif with a flavour of oranges and gentian. Evocatively French. On its own, syrupy and heavy, but wonderfully refreshing when served with a spot of grenadine, a little soda, several large ice cubes, and a slice of orange.

- **Amontillado (g)** 15.5–18% Second among the principal classifications of *Sherry*. An amontillado is darker than a fino, and should have a dry but powerful and often nutty flavour. Serve with soup courses, or as a hospitable greeting, or chilled as an apéritif.

Amoroso (g) 18–24% A rich, sweetened version of the *Oloroso* sherry. Serve at room temperature to sweet-toothed guests, as an afternoon drink with fruit cake or desserts, or after dinner.

Anejo The Spanish word for old is sometimes applied to a very fine, aged rum worthy of the respect implied by after-dinner drinking.

Anesone (g) 45% Italian aniseed and liquorice flavoured drink similar to French *Absinthe* substitutes and Greek *Ouzo*.

- **Angostura (p)** 39% The most famous patent bitters. Originally made in the town of Angostura, Venezuela, and now produced in Trinidad. Formulated by a military doctor in the Caribbean, with gentian as its most pronounced ingredient. Many cocktail and culinary uses, and as the "pink" for gin.

Anis (g) Term broadly used to cover all aniseed flavoured drinks, but more specifically referring to liqueurs with varying degrees of sweetness. In Spain, where the local *Absinthe* replacement is known as ojen (g), the term anis specifically means a liqueur of the syrupy type. These liqueurs, which are very popular in Spain, are available in both sweet and dry forms.

nisette (g) 25–30% French name for a sweet, aniseed-flavoured liqueur. The most famous producer is Marie Brizard.

péritif (g) A broad and a narrow meaning, and no accent in English. Broadly, any alcoholic drink which may be taken before a meal to sharpen the appetite: well-hopped ales, dry champagne, dry sherries, most of the classic cocktails, dry vermouths. More specifically, the term apéritif is used to describe patent drinks that are made especially for this purpose. Most, but not all, of these are pink or dark red. Their alcoholic content is usually around 20%. Some are a development of the vermouth idea. These include *Byrrh*, *Dubonnet*, *Lillet*, *St Raphael*, all from France; and *Punt e Mes*, from Italy. Others are a gentle form of bitters, including *Amer Picon* from France, and *Campari* from Italy.

pollinaris (p) What *Perrier* is to France, Apollinaris is to Germany. It is the country's best-known mineral water, and its red-triangle trademark (similar to that of Bass beer) enjoys widespread recognition. It is naturally carbonated, but much less so than Perrier. It has a high mineral content, and its alkaline composition makes it an excellent soother of hangovers. The source is at Bad Neuenahr, in a wine-producing area downstream from Koblenz.

pple brandy (g) See *Applejack* and *Calvados*.

pplejack (g) 45–50% An apple brandy is the main ingredient of several cocktails and long drinks, and in North America it may well have to be applejack. At the lower strength, it will be blended with neutral alcohol, at the higher it will be straight. The United States is one of the world's two important producers of apple brandies, the other being France, where the drink is known generically as eaux-de-vie de cidre. The greatest of these French apple brandies is *Calvados*, produced within an appellation reglementée region of Normandy.

pricot brandy (g) In many countries, products labelled as apricot brandy are made by the infusion of the fruit in a spirit base. Although this type of product is perfectly reputable, and is

offered by most of the major distillers in Europe
it is not a brandy; it is a liqueur, usually with an
alcohol content in the 20–35% range. In the
United States, the government has created a
category known as the flavoured brandy. While
some of the European products are based on
neutral alcohol, and others on grape brandy,
only the latter is permitted in this American category, and alcohol content must be a minimum of
35%. A true apricot brandy is not based on anything; it is distilled from the fruit. The most
famous example is *Barack Pálinka* (p) 40%,
which originates from Hungary and is made by
the firm of Zwack in Vienna. Hungary still produces a fine Kecskemét apricot brandy. Similar
confusion over production methods exists in the
case of other fruit brandies, but to a lesser
extent because of special generic terms which
often identify the distilled product. Apples are
distilled into *applejack* or *Calvados*, cherries into
Kirsch, plums into *Quetsch*, *Mirabelle* or *Slivovitz*. See separate entries.

- **Apricot liqueurs (g)** See above. Also *Abricotine* and
  Apry.

Apry (p) 30–35% Apricot liqueur of excellent quality
made by Marie Brizard.

Aquavit (g) 35–50% Although the best-known brand
worldwide is Danish (see akvavit), both Sweden
and Norway produce spirits of this type. Norway's most famous brand, *Linie* (p), derives its
name from an extraordinary tradition. The name
means line, and refers to the Equator. Norwegian
seafaring tradition demands that the best aquavit
should spend some time at sea before being
drunk, and Linie crosses the Equator twice on a
journey to and from Australia before being put
on sale. Each bottle is marked with the name of
the ship on which it travelled, and the date of the
voyage. The motion of the ship, the changes in
temperature during the voyage, and the salt
breezes are supposed to contribute to the
characteristic softness of Linie aquavit. Although
Swedish aquavit is the least known internationally, it enjoys the largest home market. The state
monopoly produces about 20 varieties, including
the caraway type, which the rest of the world
most readily recognizes as aquavit, but the best-
seller locally is an unflavoured brand. Although
the Swedes use the term aquavit, they more commonly refer to hard liquor as brännvin. See also
Swedish Punsch.

Armagnac (g) 40% The world's second great brandy, which the French have managed to keep largely to themselves. Although both cognac and armagnac come from the south-west of France, their centres of production are about 150 miles apart. The cognac-producing area lies well to the north of the town of Bordeaux, and reaches out to the coast; the armagnac country lies well to the south of Bordeaux, and reaches out towards the mountains. It is an area flavoured by those mountains, the Pyrenees, and by the influences of Basque and Gascon history, and its famous brandy is produced in the départements of Gers and Les Landes. While the countryside of Cognac is gentle, that of Armagnac is hilly and hot; Cognac has chalky soil, Armagnac has sandy soil; the Cognac grape is usually the St Emilion, the Armagnac grape, the folle blanche. While cognac is double-distilled in pot stills, armagnac is single-distilled in its own hybrid variety of still. It is also produced to a lower alcoholic content (and therefore more flavour) before being aged and blended. Cognac is aged in Limousin or Tronçais oak; Armagnac gains some of its flavour from the dark, sappy, tannic Monlezun oak. At its best, cognac has sophistication and finesse; armagnac is rich and pungent. Cognac is universally recognized as the most elegant of all spirits, but armagnac is prized and in some cases preferred by connoisseurs of brandy. It is said, rather fancifully, to have been the brandy of d'Artagnan, and it is certainly mentioned in French history 200 years before cognac. Yet for many years most armagnacs went north to be blended into cognac, in which their colour and character created an illusion of greater age. Today, the ages of armagnacs are indicated by the same labelling practices as those which apply to cognac. The best-quality brandies come from Bas-Armagnac and Ténarèze, although the biggest of the producing zones is Haut-Armagnac. While cognac is dominated in the world market by big names such as Bisquit, Courvoisier, Martell, Hennessy, Hine and Rémy Martin, the production and marketing of armagnac is for the moment much more fragmented.

Arak, arrak, arrack (g) Eastern word, of Arabic origin, describing any distilled spirit. An arak may be any Eastern spirit, from an aniseed or liquorice-flavoured liquor in the style of raki (a related word) to a pungent rum. It may be distilled from grape, grain, date or the sap of the coconut palm. The most famous, Batavia Arrak, is made in Java, Indonesia, from malted rice and molasses, and is aged for between seven and ten years. See *Swedish Punsch*.

Asbach (p) 40% The best known of the German brandies, produced on the Rhine at Rüdesheim. Like cognac, the good-quality German brandies are aged in wood, usually Limousin oak. Well-known producers include Dujardin and Scharlachberg. A brandy conforming to the highest national standards in Germany is labelled as a weinbrand in the local market. A lesser confection may be called only a branntwein aus wein.

Asti Important Italian wine-growing region to the east of Turin, in the province of Piedmont. Famous for Asti Spumante, a sweet and fruity sparkling wine, of low alcohol content, made from moscato grapes.

Aurum (p) 40% An unusual golden-coloured liqueur of herbs and fruit with a sharp tang of orange peel, based on brandy. Produced at Pescara, Italy. The Aurum distillery company also produces other liqueurs.

B and B (p) 43% "Bénédictine and Brandy" liqueur. Although *Bénédictine* itself is based on cognac, it is sometimes taken with brandy; a slug of hard liquor knocks the sweetness off many a liqueur, while retaining the distinctive flavour. A "B and B" is said to have been a popular order in North America long before the Bénédictine company put both drinks into one bottle, in 1938. By doing so, they ensured that their precious liqueur was not sullied with inferior brandies, and they made the profit on the cognac.

Bacardi (p) Old-established firm of rum producers who moved from Cuba to Puerto Rico, and now have distilleries in several other places. Bacardi did much to popularize light-bodied rums during the 1960s. The name Bacardi was commonly used to describe a cocktail, a grenadine version of the Daiquiri, until the firm took legal steps to protect its trademark.

Bailey's Irish Cream (p) 15%+ A distinctive chocolate-flavoured whiskey and double cream liqueur of low alcohol content produced in the Republic of Ireland. Formulated in the 1970s, and one of the few totally new drinks to have enjoyed considerable success.

Banana liqueurs Crème de banane **(g)** 25–30% is made in many countries. Bananas are macerated in neutral spirit, or artificial flavourings are used. An excellent banana liquer is made in the Canary Islands from local fruit. The bottle is shaped like a bunch of bananas.

Barack Pálinka (p) see *Apricot brandy*.

Barbados rums (g) 40%+ Good-quality, medium-light rums with a distinctively smoky flavour made by both pot and continuous stills. Some very well aged. See *Rum*.

Beerenburg (g) Approx 30% The national drink of Friesland, according to the Dutch. Although the long-lost European nation of Friesland is now largely shared between The Netherlands and Germany, it clings to its own traditions. Beerenburg was named after an Amsterdam herb and spice merchant but it was, and still is, the distinctive bitters of the Dutch province of Friesland. It is made from 15 herbs, including violet roots, angelica roots, gentian and bay leaves, and its alcohol content varies depending upon the producer. In that part of Friesland which is in Germany, the "national" drink is *Friesengeist*, a unique mint-flavoured spirit.

Bénédictine (p) 43% Sometimes described as the world's oldest liqueur, because it was formulated in 1510. The particular Bénédictines who devised this elixir had an abbey in the little seaside town of Fécamp, in the Caux district of Normandy. The abbey was sacked during the French Revolution, but in 1863 the formula for the liqueur providentially came into the hands of a local merchant, Alexandre le Grand, who is said to have been a descendant of a trustee of the abbey. After tireless effort and experiment, he finally managed to produce the liqueur with such commercial success that he was able to build a "palace" and art museum which is today a great tourist attraction. "To God Most Good, Most Great," says the Bénédictine dedication Deo Optimo Maximo, which is initialled on every bottle. Twenty-seven of God's herbs, plants and peels go into Bénédictine, and some of them blossom on the cliffs nearby. The extraction, by steeping and maceration, of essences and flavours is a matter for great attention; the processes are many and complicated; a certain sequence must be followed; and production takes three years, followed by four years of ageing. Bénédictine is typical of the drink made by a secret formula. Innumerable imitators have failed to copy it convincingly, and the Germans have a whole genus of "Diktiner". It is for its individuality of character as much as its antiquity that Bénédictine has become one of the world's most famous liqueurs. If any other enjoys a comparable reputation, then that must be *Chartreuse*.

Bianco Italian word for white. Often used as a generic term for the white variety of sweet Italian vermouth (16%), which has a tinge of vanilla in its taste. Although both bianco and rosso (red) are sweet, the latter is slightly less so, due to the influence of absinthe gentilia. Dry white vermouth is identified simply as secco.

Bitter (g) Familiar term used in Britain for everyday beer. Usually refers to a draught beer, always of the top-fermented type. Some of these beers have a pronounced hop bitterness, others are maltier. Traditionally, all British brewers produce a bitter (3–5.5%) and a mild (3–4.25%), but many have run down the latter. Unpasteurized bitters are demanded by connoisseurs.

• **Bitter stout (g)** Guinness (p) is the classic example. Murphy's (p) and Beamish (p), both brewed in Cork, Ireland, are also excellent bitter, or dry, stouts, and there are a few such beers elsewhere in the world. Bitter stouts (4–7.5%) have a far higher hopping rate, and a higher alcoholic content, than sweet stouts, of which Mackeson (p) is the classic example. See *Stout*.

Bitters (g) Wide-ranging term for bitter essences and alcoholic drinks made from roots, flowers, fruits and peels macerated in neutral spirit. Common ingredients include orange, gentian and quinine. Apart from orange and peach bitters for use in the cocktail bar, there are innumerable patent potions, in several quite different categories: the dash of bitters (35–40%), which may be *Angostura* (Trinidadian), *Peychaud* (Franco-American) or even hangover-curing *Underberg* (German), the bitter apéritif which fraternizes with the vermouths, typical examples being *Amer Picon* (21%) from France, and *Campari* (24%) from Italy; the versatile apéritif-or-digestif type of 40%+, which might also double as a hangover cure, like *Fernet Branca* from Italy and sometimes France, or *Jägermeister* from Germany; and the contrarily sweet bitters of 30%+, such as Italian *China-Martini* or Spanish *Calisay*.

Blackberry Liqueurs (approx 30%) are made by the maceration of blackberries in spirit or brandy. Sometimes red wine or *Eau-de-vie* is added. The

Polish *Jerzynowka* (p) is a good example. Silesia gave birth to a distinctive liqueur of wild blackberries called *Kroatzbeere*. The original makers, prefixing their product with the word *Echte* ("the real thing"), now produce Kroatzbeere (p) in West Germany. It avoids the sickly sweetness of many liqueurs, has an excellent bouquet, and an alcohol content of 30%.

Blackcurrant Several blackcurrant liqueurs are made in different parts of the world, but the most famous come from France, from the Dijon area, where they are known as crème de *Cassis* (g). These Burgundian cassis liqueurs (15%+) are made by the maceration of blackcurrants in neutral spirit or *Eau-de-vie*. Small quantities of other berry fruits and sugar may be added. Burgundian cassis is widely used as a mixer, with chilled white wine, *Champagne* and *Vermouth*, to produce a typically French apéritif, or with *Cognac* to create a rich after-dinner drink. Blackcurrants are also distilled into a true brandy of about 45%, known as eau-de-vie de cassis.

Blended whisky, whiskey The biggest-selling scotches on both sides of the Atlantic are blends, and this is likely to be true of any whisky that doesn't trouble to say otherwise. The Scots blend the cheaper but relatively tasteless continuous still grain whiskies with the more expensive and distinctive pot still malts to produce a compromise on both price and palate. In the United States, a distiller may blend several straight whiskeys with each other, or with a lesser whiskey, or with neutral spirit.

Bock, double bock (g) 6–13% The strongest style of lager beer, associated with Munich though the name is probably a corruption of Einbeck, a town in Lower Saxony. Although bock is seasonal (spring and autumn), its customary goat label has nothing to do with Capricorn. Bock means billy-goat in German. Perversely, the Belgians and French describe a weak beer in a large glass as bock.

Bols (p) Popularly associated with their old Hollands gin, which comes in a stoneware crock, Bols are an internationally known drinks company making a large range of typically Dutch products. In addition to that stonily proud "Z.O.Genever", Bols produce a number of other Dutch gins, old, young and flavoured, under various brandnames, and a large selection of liqueurs, many of which originated in The Netherlands. These include *curaçao*, crème de cacao, parfait amour, and esoteric specialities such as Tip van Bootz and Hansje in de kelder. Lucas Bols, who went into business in Amsterdam in 1575, may have been the world's first commercial distiller. Among the several other important Dutch gin and liqueur firms, only De Kuyper has a substantial name outside The Netherlands, although there are many excellent small houses. See *Jenever*.

Boonekamp (p) 35% A *Bitters* which lives up to that description with a dry, daunting determination. Its forename is Petrus, and its surname is pronounced bone-a-camp. Its formula dates back to 1743 and is Dutch, but Boonekamp later became a German taste, and now enjoys a particular reputation among the bitter-bibbers of Italy.

Bordeaux (g) See *Claret*.

Borovicka (g) 35–40% Eastern European spirit of the gin family, similar in style to German *Steinhäger*. See *Gin*.

• **Bourbon (g)** 40–50% It was in Bourbon County, Kentucky, then a territory not a state, that America first managed to produce a really drinkable whiskey from corn. One account says a distiller called John Ritchie completed this act of alchemy at Linn's Fort, east of Bardstown in 1777, but popular legend favours the Reverend Elijah Craig, of Georgetown, and the year 1789. The Scottish and Irish settlers on the Eastern seaboard had distilled whisk(e)y from barley, as in their home countries, but as they pushed inland to settle new territory, they found it easier to grow other grains. First came rye, then the corn (maize) of Bourbon County. The whiskey territories were well found, for spring water presented itself through the limestone shelf which underpins parts of Maryland and Pennsylvania (the great rye whiskey states), the Virginias, Indiana, Illinois and Kentucky. Even today, more than half the bourbon distilleries of the United States are in Kentucky. Bourbon whiskey must contain at least 51% corn, and in practice is likely to contain 60 or 80%, with additional proportions of rye and barley. The two classic American whiskeys are both produced in continuous stills, and matured in new, charred white-oak barrels for not less than a year. A straight whiskey must be aged for at least two years, although most are matured for far longer. All straight whiskeys are aged and bottled in bonded warehouses. Bourbon and rye greatly lack the subtlety and sophistication of scotch and Irish, but that is not their métier. They have an almost fruity sweetness and a very full flavour, partly because they are distilled off at a lower alcohol content, and their palate is influenced by the charred oak. Instead of finesse, they have robustness. They are a different spirit, of a different time and place. See *Rye, Tennessee whiskey, Sour mash, Corn whiskey, Light whiskey* and *Malt whiskey.*

Brandy (g) 40–50% In several languages, the word for spirits derives from the word meaning to burn. The allusion is not necessarily to firewater, but the the process of distillation itself. The first distillers were seen to apply fire to various liquids, apparently to burn them until they vanished in vapour before being reconstituted in a different form. In the languages of northern Europe, to brand is to burn. Brandy has come to mean a distillate, although not of grain but of fruit. Any fruit, having been fermented and then distilled, is a brandy. Any spirit distilled from fruit is a brandy. All the famous fruit distillates of Alsace and the neighbouring parts of Germany and Switzerland, what the French call eaux-de-vie (and in so doing pick up another linguistic thread in the description of spirits), are all brandies, whether they are made from cherries into kirsch, from an endless assortment of berries, or from various plums. If a fermented mash of apples is distilled, that is a brandy, whether or not it is entitled by the place of its birth also to be a calvados. If grape skins are distilled into marc (or grappa, or tresterschnapps, or whatever), that is a brandy of sorts. Most conventionally, a wine distillate is a brandy, whether it be humble and homeless or a haughty armagnac or a fine champagne cognac. "Brandy" with no further qualification has therefore come to mean a grape distillate. What is not a brandy is a neutral spirit which has been flavoured with fruit; that is a liqueur.

See *Cognac, Armagnac, Calvados, Eau-de-vie.*

Bristol Cream (p) Brand name of a very fine *Oloroso* sherry shipped by Harvey's, of Bristol.

Brown sherry (g) Imprecise term used in British markets to indicate a particularly dark and sweet *Oloroso.*

Brut (g) A bone-dry *Champagne* without the customary *dosage* of sugar-sweetened wine. This *dosage* varies between 1% and 10%, depending upon the type of champagne being made. After brut, in descending order of dryness, come extra sec or extra dry (in reality, just dry), sec (slightly sweet), demi-sec (sweet), doux (very sweet).

Burgundy (g) If Champagne is set aside as a special case, then France's two greatest wine regions are Bordeaux (see *Claret*) and Burgundy. In the centre of eastern France, Burgundy was a kingdom in the Middle Ages, and it remains politically an important region. With Dijon as its main town, it is almost as famous for its gastronomy as for its rich, sonorous red wines. Burgundy popularly means red, but the region also has many white wines, including the great Chablis. Its wine-growing areas, and just a sampling of their famous districts, are: Beaujolais (Fleurie), Mâcon (Pouilly-Fuissé), Chalon (Montagny), Beaune (Montrachet), Côte de Nuits (Nuits-St-Georges, Gevrey-Chambertin), and Chablis. The principal grapes of Burgundy are the Pinot Noir and the Chardonnay.

Byrrh (p) 17% French patent apéritif of the vermouth type, dryish and of medium weight, with a kiss of orange and quinine.

• **Cacao, crème de (g)** 25–30% Chocolate liqueur produced in colourless and brown versions, the latter sometimes also flavoured with vanilla. The word Chouao on the label means the cacao beans come from Venezuela. Chouao is a suburb of Caracas. Crème de cacao is useful in both the cocktail bar and the kitchen, and is a popular drink in the Marseilles area. It is sometimes drunk through a layer of cream.

Calisay (p) 33% The speciality of Catalonia, and a liqueur well known throughout Spain. Made in Barcelona to a recipe which is said to have originated in Bohemia, Calisay is a slightly syrupy quinine liqueur. It is sometimes chilled as an apéritif, but works better as an after-dinner drink. Calisay is also used in desserts and cakes.

Calvados (g) 40–50% One of the world's great brandies, the finest of apple distillates, and a proud speciality of Normandy, with its own appellation contrôlée and réglementée regions. The finest calvados come from the appellation contrôlée region known as Pays d'Auge, and is double-distilled in a pot still before being aged for at least one year. In practice, it is usually matured for several years, in oak casks. Good calvados is very dry and smooth, with a subtle bouquet. Not only is it drunk after meals but also as a refresher between courses by the delightfully gluttonous Normans. Lest their palates should momentarily forget the apple, they also use calvados extensively in their formidable cuisine. The département of Calvados is said to have taken its name from a galleon of the Spanish Armada which was wrecked on the Normandy coast as it fled from Sir Francis Drake. Apple brandy from outside the calvados appellation réglementée region may be called only eau-de-vie de cidre de Normandie (or Bretagne, or Maine, or wherever).

Campari (p) 24% Internationally, the best-known Italian patent apéritif. Commonly drunk on the rocks with soda, and the basis of two famous cocktails, the Americano and the Negroni. Campari is very dry, with a pronounced quinine taste. In Italy, visiting professors of Campari find it hard to avoid the rather weak pre-mixed soda version. Half the fun lies in getting the mix just right, and contemplating the rich, translucent red liquid as it refracts the midday sun.

Campbeltown malt whisky (g) 40–45%+ From Kintyre, lately famous for McCartney's Mull. Among Scotland's recognized whisky-producing regions (*Highland, Lowland, Islay, Island*). Campbeltown is the smallest. It is nothing more than a very small town, but it once had more than 30 distilleries. Campbeltown was then Scotland's whisky capital, and Kintyre in the south-west more famous than Speyside in the north-east. Then the town wrecked its own reputation by producing a spate of poor whiskies to meet sudden demand from desperate Americans during Prohibition. Today, Campbeltown has only two distilleries, producing excellent whiskies but each of a rather different character. If today's Campbeltown whiskies have anything in common, it is that they form a bridge between the Lowland and Islay malts. Glen Scotia is peaty but also oily. Springbank is light but with a very full palate.

Canadian whisky (g) 32.5–43.5% Of the American type, but much lighter in body, crisper and less assertive than the whiskeys of the United States. The less anonymous among the Canadians have a light tang of rye. Canadian distillers commonly use malted rye as well as a high proportion of rye grain, together with the usual corn and malted barley, but their whiskies are blended with grain spirit that has been rectified to the point of

neutrality. The actual style of whisky to be produced in Canada is the one aspect ignored in an
edifice of regulations concerning the production
(and sale) of liquor in the Dominion, and brands
vary considerably. Both old and new casks are
used for ageing, which must last for three years
although six or eight is more common.

Cane spirit (g) Predictably, South Africa's alleged
national spirit is "white". It is also tasteless. A
rectified rum or a vodka distilled from sugar
cane, depending upon the way you look at it.

Cassis, crème de (g) See *Blackcurrant*. A quite different cassis is a lively white wine from Provence.
The two can be mixed to advantage.

Chablis (g) One of the world's greatest dry white
wines, from *Burgundy*, although elsewhere in the
world the name is applied to products which bear
no resemblance to the original. A greeny-gold
wine of which Hugh Johnson says in *The World
Atlas of Wine*: "It is hard but not harsh, reminds
one of stones and minerals, but at the same time
of green hay."

• **Chartreuse (p)** 55% green, 40% yellow Of the famous
herbal liqueurs, this is the most sophisticated.
Such rich and aromatic elixirs are perhaps an
acquired after-dinner taste, but their inscru-
tability is quite provocative. The Carthusian
brothers assure us that their basic "elixir vegetal"
and its derivative liqueurs, despite their memor-
able colours, contain not even the most innocent
of dyes, but merely 130 herbs and spices which
are variously infused, macerated and distilled,
and then aged for some years in enormous oak
casks, watched over by monks. Chartreuse even
continues to mature very slowly in the bottle.
"Exceptionally well-aged" versions are sometimes produced. Chartreuse is the oldest among
those liqueurs which are still produced by monks,
and it has the obligatory romantic story. The
formula dates back to the 16th century, but the
process was not perfected until 1764, and commercial production did not begin until 1848.
There were various alarums and excursions, and
at one stage the monks were exiled to Spain,
where they began a distillery which still operates
in Tarragona. That establishment is visited once
a year by the only three monks from France
who know the formula. The main distillery is
15 miles from the monastery of Chartreuse,
which itself is in wooded countryside in the foot-
hills of the French Alps, near Grenoble. Chart-

reuse is commercially marketed by a lay company. There are many liqueurs vertes and liqueurs jaunes which affect a similar style, and the Germans have what they call "Kartäuser" digestifs.

hampagne (g) In order to be worth drinking from a pretty girl's shoe, sparkling wine must not only have been grown within cork-popping distance of Rheims and Epernay, but must also have been made by the champagne method. Champagne is a region nearly 100 miles north-east of Paris, around Rheims and Epernay, with outposts in the Aube département; the champagne method is a means of imparting the sparkle by secondary fermentation in the bottle, not in a large tank, and—perish the thought—not by artificial carbonation. If either of the first two methods is used, the sparkle will persist in the glass, but artificial carbonation produces only the most ephemeral spasm of excitement. A good champagne, a blend of Pinot Noir and Chardonnay grapes, may take eight years or more to reach maturity. Showmanship aside, it should not pop noisily, but merely utter the sigh of a satisfied woman. A good champagne has a tantalizing combination of delicate beauty and racy promise. It should be thoroughly cooled, but not icy. Good sparkling wines, vins mousseux, are made elsewhere in France, notably Savoy.

hampagne cognac (g) Although the soil in the best Cognac region is similar to that in Champagne, there is no connection whatever between the sparkling wine and the brandy. *Champaigne* is the Old French word for an expanse of open country. The cognac-producing region is divided into six districts, among which the two producing the finest brandy are called Grande and Petite Champagne. In fact, the Cognac region is on the opposite side of France from the home of champagne wine.

heri-Suisse (p) 30% Swiss liqueur reproducing the flavour of cherry-filled chocolates. To be placed gently between the cherry lips of a woman who needs a little indulgence.

herry brandy (g) Term commonly applied with some imprecision to cherry liqueurs (see *Apricot brandy*). Several styles. The Danes produce the type which has a dry tinge, a pleasing "almond" bitterness from the stone, as exemplified by Peter Heering, a brand which enjoys a considerable reputation. Several similar cherry liqueurs are produced in The Netherlands, among which

41

De Kuyper (p) is one of the best known. Although the kernel is used in maraschino, this clear cherry liqueur, with its intense flavour and flowery bouquet, is quite sweet. *Maraschino* (g) 30–40% is made from the marasca cherry of Dalmatia, and its bottle is typically encased in straw. Drioli first made maraschino in Zara when it was part of the Republic of Venice. When the area became a part of Yugoslavia, although production of maraschino has continued there, Drioli moved to the city of Venice, and the famous firm of Luxardo to Padua. The cherries are now grown in the Po Valley. Farther east, the Slavic countries also produce a cherry liqueur called wisniak (g) approx 25% and an excellent cherry-flavoured vodka, wisniowka (g) 40%. A great many countries have cherry liqueurs, sometimes several types, and the French produce and excellent pale, light version called guignole (g), in addition to a kirsch-based version, and kirsch itself, which is a true brandy.
See *Kirsch*, *Kirschwasser*.

Chianti (g) One of the best Italian wines, and certainly the most widely known, although often through imitations. The Chianti area covers most of Tuscany, and the "Classico" wines come from the lovely hills between Florence and Siena. A number of different grapes are used, but all chianti is red. In its familiar straw-wrapped flask, beloved of restaurant decorators and table lamp makers, chianti has a refreshing prickle induced by the addition of a little unfermented must of dried grapes. If it comes in a claret bottle it is untreated chianti, of the best, and has been aged in oak.

China-Martini (p) 31% The first word, pronounced rather like "keener", is a reference to the quinine in the drink. Martini and Rossi, of vermouth fame, are the makers. Despite being 180 years old, this patent liqueur is little known outside Italy, although it can now be found elsewhere, and is well worth trying. As an apéritif, it is diluted with two parts of slightly sweetened lemon juice, and perhaps a swoosh of soda, and served over ice. More commonly, it is drunk as an after-dinner liqueur. China-Martini is a slightly syrupy drink, and is said to be the only "sweet bitters" in Italy. It is also made into a toddy with hot water and lemon juice.

Chocolate Rather sweet chocolate liqueurs, sometimes with an additional flavouring of coffee mint, nuts or fruits, are made in various parts of the world. They are not be drunk until after eight in the evening. The best known is Chocolat Suisse (p). This precocious confection even contains floating chocolate pieces. In Britain, a whole range of flavoured Royal Chocolate (p) treats has been devised by a liqueur expert, Peter Hallgarten. A member of a well-known wine-shipping family, Mr Hallgarten is also the author of a much-respected study, *Spirits and Liqueurs*.

See *Cacao, crème de*.

Cinzano (p) One of the best-known *Vermouth* houses in Italy, the other being Martini and Rossi. Both are near Turin.

Claret (g) A description bestowed by the English on the graceful red wines of Bordeaux. The use of the term claret probably derives from England's rule over that part of France in the Middle Ages. Although the word is imprecise in meaning, and carries no weight or authority, it has passed into the popular terminology of alcoholic drink. Bordeaux is the biggest viticultural area of France, and no region in the world produces so much fine wine. A number of different grapes are used. Only half of Bordeaux's wine is red, and few of its famous districts are wholly monochrome in any sense of the word. Although Médoc is famous for red wines, Margaux also produces a little white; Pomerol and St Emilion are known for their reds; Graves is known for whites, but also produces red wines; Barsac and Sauternes are famous for their white wines; Entre-Deux-Mers produces mainly white. Among the famous châteaux of Bordeaux, Lafite, Latour and Mouton-Rothschild are all in Pauillac. Hugh Johnson says in *The World Atlas of Wine*: "Many claret-lovers would tell you that the wines of Pauillac have the quintessential flavour they look for in Bordeaux—a combination of fresh soft fruit, oak, dryness, subtlety combines with substance, a touch of cigar-box, a suggestion of sweetness. Even the lesser growths of Pauillac approach their ideal claret."

Cognac (g) 40% The most elegant of all spirits. To be cognac, a brandy must come from there; not from the little town of Cognac, but from the region around it, the basin of the river Charente, and the small islands off that coast, in the Bay of Biscay. The grapes grown there have never made good wine, but they make the finest brandy,

especially in the parts of Cognac with the chalkiest topsoil. The cognac-producing region is divided into six districts, among which the chalkiest is called Grande Champagne (nothing to do with the sparkling wine—see separate entry). The cognac from Grande Champagne has the greatest finesse. Then, through Petite Champagne to the district called Borderies, it has less finesse, a fuller body and a higher flavour. It becomes again less delicate, and progressively earthy, through Fins Bois, Bons Bois, and Bois Ordinaires. All cognac must be distilled twice, in pot stills, and aged for not less than two years, in oak. Most good cognacs are aged for at least three years, and usually far longer, and all are blended. A three-star label is not intended specifically to convery the age of the brandy; a three-star cognac is likely to be the firm's standard brand, its youngest and cheapest blend. A five-star label has precise meaning. No cognac of less than four and a half years may be used in a brand which is labelled VSOP (these initials stand for Very Special Old Pale, in English, and evidence the historical importance of trade with Albion). These cognacs are sometimes labelled réserve, or described as liqueur brandy. They are not liqueurs as understood by the English, but in the French sense of a fine after-dinner drink. A "Napoléon" brandy must be at least five years old, and this grandiose style has no more meaning than that, whatever else may be implied. Some firms produce a "Napoléon" and then a slightly older blend, with a shoulder full of epithets: grand réserve, extra réserve, extra vieille, très vieille, cordon bleu, cordon argent, age inconnu. The last seems rather disingenuous, since brandy deteriorates after about 70 years in the cask. In the bottle, it does not age at all.
See *Armagnac* and *Eau-de-vie*.

Cointreau (p) 40% The world's best-known brand of *triple sec* (g) from a well-regarded liqueur house in France. Triple sec is a type of colourless *Curaçao* (g), which is a liqueur made from the peel of small green oranges native to the island of that name in the former Dutch West Indies (Netherlands Antilles). The house of Cointreau pioneered curaçao, which is also a speciality among Dutch distillers.

Continuous Still A mixed blessing, since its talent for the light-bodied or even tasteless spirit, its efficiency and economy, and its ability to produce the same product irrespective of location or surroundings, place a terrible temptation before liquor producers and marketers. The continuous still in its various forms is also known as the column, patent or Coffey still. It derives from the efficient continuous sytem of distillation pioneered in Scotland by Robert Stein and Aeneas Coffey in the late 1820s and early 1830s. Although Coffey was a former Inspector-General of Excise in Ireland, his invention was not acceptable there, so he emigrated to Scotland. The Coffey still is used there today in the production of grain whisky, but the *Pot Still* is used for malt whiskies, cognac, French fruit brandies and most spirits of great character.

Cordial (g) In the United States, a synonym for liqueur. Although the word cordial may be more commonly applied to American products and liqueur than to those from Europe, both in that context describe the same thing. The maker of a cordial/liqueur begins with a ready-made spirit base, in which he then infuses, macerates, or redistils flavouring agents. These may be roots, barks, flowers, fruits, or a mixture of several. The legal definition of a cordial or liqueur often says that it must be sweetened. Cordials and liqueurs are most commonly taken after dinner, and in many cases have a modest alcohol content. A redistillation of alcohol with herbs or fruit to produce a strong, dry drink is regarded as a flavoured vodka or aquavit.

Corenwijn (g) 40% A distinctive Dutch grain spirit of the highest quality, which might popularly be regarded as a .type of schnapps. The base of corenwijn (corn wine) is rye, maize and barley in equal proportions. It is triple distilled, and aged for several years in wood, but retains its own characteristic palate. Drink ice-cold, straight up, in a small Dutch gin or liqueur glass. Goes well as an appetizer with a salt herring.

Corn whiskey (g) Approx 40% An American rural whiskey containing not less than 80 per cent corn, and aged in uncharred barrels. Although a bourbon is also made from corn, it may contain a lower percentage (minimum 51 per cent), and it must be aged in charred barrels. The latter is a particularly important distinction.
See *Bourbon, Rye, Tennessee.*

Cow (g) Milk or cream-based liqueur of low alcoholic strength, for inexperienced drinkers or milk shakes. Invented in the 1970s.

Cream sherry (g) A dark, smooth sweet *Oloroso*.

Crème de (g) Liqueur in which one flavour predominates. Usually very sweet. The term does not necessarily imply that the liqueur contains or resembles cream.

Cuban rum (g) 40%+ Light-bodied rum used in the Daiquiri cocktail, which was named after a Cuban tin-mining town. Carta Blanca (p) is the main "white" brand and the golden Carta Oro (p) is coloured with caramel. The light style of rum, made in continuous stills, is extensively produced in Puerto Rico.

Cuarenta y Tres (p) 34% Forty-three ingredients go into this brandy-based patent liqueur, which is very popular in its native Spain. Sweetish, with a vanilla plate.

•**Curaçao (g)** 25–40% The only generic orange liqueur. All the others are proprietary brands. Curaçao is made in several different degrees of dryness, the best known of which is *triple sec*, made with distinction by the French house of *Cointreau*. Since the small, green, bitter oranges which donate their peel to the drink grow on the island of Curaçao, in the former Dutch West Indies (Netherlands Antilles), the liqueurists of Holland usually include several variations in their ranges. Although curaçao appears in a variety of colours, these strange hues have nothing to do with its taste, and merely serve a splendidly decorative purpose, especially in mixed drinks.

Cusenier (p) Well-regarded and long-established French liqueur house, noted for its Freezomint (p) green crème de menthe.

Cynar (p) 17% Artichoke-based patent aperitif made in Italy, where it is well known. Efficacious and excellent, unlikely though it may sound. Serve with two or three cubes of ice, and a swoosh of soda.

D.O.M. See *Bénédictine*.

Daniel's, Jack (p) See *Jack Daniel's*.

Danziger Goldwasser (g) 30–40% The most spectacular of liqueurs in which glistening flecks of gold-leaf float like a heaven-sent snowstorm. The gold is perfectly edible; indeed, it was originally added for its allegedly therapeutic properties. Goldwassers are flavoured with caraway, aniseed and sometimes orange peel. The original was made in Danzig (now Gdansk, Poland) by the firm of Der Lachs (p), now based in West Berlin. Goldwasser is one of the oldest liqueurs, and has a brother called silberwasser. Drinks of this type are popular among liqueur houses elsewhere in Europe, and the Dutch also have a version called Bruidstranen, "Bride's Tears".

Digestif (g) That the French should have a noun, and the English language conventionally an adjective, says much about the respective values of the two cultures. A digestif is an after-dinner drink. If it is not a mellow brandy or a gentlemanly port, then it may well be a patent potion of mint, caraway or Chinese rhubarb which would be an altogether less agreeable experience if taken in pharmaceutical form.

Dortmunder (g) 5%+ Style of German *Lager* beer which is less bitter than *Pilsener* but more bitter than *Münchener*. Sometimes known in Germany as Export. Dortmund is Germany's biggest brewing city.

Drambuie (p) 40% The oldest and most famous whisky liqueur, said to be produced from Bonnie Prince Charlie's own recipe, which was allegedly given to the present makers in return for their assistance to him. Drambuie, which means "the drink that satisfies" in Gaelic, is made from Highland malt whisky and heather honey. There are several other liqueurs based on scotch, among which *Glayva*, made with herbs and spices, is the best known. Glen Mist is an excellent honey-flavoured Scotch liqueur, a little drier than its competitors. There is also an excellent *Irish Mist* produced across the water.

Dubonnet (p) 17% Outside its home country, Dubonnet is the best known of the French patent apéritifs, with a deservedly high reputation. Although all the vermouth-style apéritifs are bitter-sweet, each has a different position in the taste spectrum, and Dubonnet stands right in the middle. Its first taste is sweet, but it becomes smooth, with a tinge of quinine. The rich red kind is best known, but a blonde version is popular in the United States.

Eau-de-vie (g) "Water of life." The French generic term for all brandies. A grape brandy, whether haughty or humble, is an eau-de-vie, although it is not normally ordered as such in a French bar. If it is not ordered by its brand-name or region or origin, then it is identified simply as a *fine*, meaning the house eau-de-vie de vin. Since *Cognac* and *Armagnac* enjoy such pre-eminence in France, the lesser eaux-de-vie de vin often make themselves scarce, skipping overseas and calling themselves simply "French grape brandy". Among those that stay at home, the considerable authority Cyril Ray has a kind word for the grape brandy of the Champagne wine region, *fine de la Marne*. There are other interesting *fines*, and a variety of grapey oddities, all worth a try in the cause of experience. The term eau-de-vie also covers a brandy made from grape skins, *Marc*, but that is really a different animal. The great apple brandy *Calvados* is an eau-de-vie de cidre, although this general term is in practice only applied to its less esteemed brothers. In the absence of any qualification, eau-de-vie would most readily be taken to mean one of the superb fruit brandies for which Alsace is especially famous. These distinctive distillates are also known as alcools blancs, because they are colourless, having been aged not in wood but in glass or pottery. They are produced not only in Alsace but also across the borders in the Black Forest area of Germany and the north of Switzerland. Every available fruit is used, and among the best-known eaux-de-vie are those distilled from cherries (*Kirsch*), pears (*Poire William* in French, birngeist in German), Switzen plums (*Quetsch*, zwetschenwasser), *Mirabelle* plums, raspberries (*Framboise*, Himbeergeist), strawberries (*Fraise, Erdbeergeist*) and gentian (*Enzian*), the last very popular in Germany and Switzerland. These eaux-de-vie are distilled in pot stills to an alcohol content of 38–45%, usually higher rather than lower. Schladerer is a large producer of excellent fruit brandies, but much of the business is in the hands of very small firms and home-distillers. Fruit eaux-de-vie are rather expensive, but they are eminently worth trying.

Echte German word for real. Sometimes used on labels of drinks to indicate "the real thing, from the original source". The word urquell is used with the same intention.

Enzian German word for gentian, the roots and flowers of which are extensively used in liqueurs. See *Eau-de-vie*.

Erdbeer German word for strawberry.

Evian French spa town at foot of Mont Blanc which produces one of the best-known mineral waters.

Falernum (g) A Caribbean syrup of mixed fruits, containing very little alcohol, which is sometimes used to flavour and sweeten mixed drinks. Lime and ginger are pronounced ingredients. Confusingly, named after a famous wine of ancient times which survives in more modest form as the Falerno (both red and white) of modern Italy.

Fernet (p) 45% A distinctive and very bitter herbal digestif made by Martini and Rossi, the vermouth specialists, in Turin. Its makers claim that theirs was the original of its type, and that rivals Branca, of Milan, followed them six months later. Such disputes are lost in the 1800s, when the mass-marketing of drink had its battle-scarred beginnings, but the Milanese Fernet-Branca is today the better known internationally. Both drinks are excellent, if acquired tastes, but they are apt to be treated in some countries exclusively as hangover cures. In that, they work on the principle of tasting so powerfully bitter that the victim can feel only better once he has swallowed them.
See *Bitters*.

Finlandia (p) 47% A strong Western-style *Vodka* marketed in a distinctively icy looking bottle. Although *Aquavit* and vodka are of the same genus, Finland is geographically perfectly placed to fill any gap between them. The Finns' other drinks are a wide and esoteric range of colourful berry liqueurs.

Fino (g) 17–18% The finest category of *Sherry*. Pale, delicate, distinctive, dry. A wonderful apéritif.

Fior d'Alpi (g) 40% The twig in the bottle, gathering sugar crystals, adds a touch of colour to these sweet liqueurs made from Alpine herbs. Mille Fiori is the same type of liqueur.

Forbidden Fruit (p) 32% Tempting and tangy old-established American liqueur made from the shaddock grapefruit, with orange and honey, and based on brandy. Splendid spherical bottle.

Fraise The French word for strawberry. Usually denotes a strawberry brandy (see *Eau-de-vie*), but also to be found on liqueurs and even a flavoured *Vermouth*.

Framboise French word for raspberry, on the labels of *Eau-de-vie* and *Crème de* framboises.

"French" Once a popular term in England, and sometimes still used, for a dry *Vermouth*. To request simply a "gin and French" was to invite a measure of dry vermouth with the liquor. Originally, French vermouths were dry and Italians sweet, but both countries have long produced both styles.

Friesengeist (p) 45% From the Frisian part of Germany, a powerful mint liqueur made by a small private firm. Frisian coffee is made not with milk from the region's famous cows but with this mighty mint, flambéed.

Fundador (p) 40% Outside Spain, probably the best-known Spanish brandy, and widely drunk in its home country. A good-quality label from the respected house of Domecq.

• **Galliano (p)** 40% Mister H. Wallbanger made it famous in the United States by his curious deeds, but this swaggering liqueur from Lombardy has long been known in Europe, and is itself named after a famous man, an Italian war hero from the conflict with the Abyssinians in the 1890s. Major Giuseppe Galliano held out for 44 days at Fort Enda, which is depicted on the label, before being forced to surrender. In his memory was named this sweetish liqueur, golden in colour, flowery, spicy, herbal, with a tinge of vanilla. Galliano is used increasingly in mixed drinks and its proud, tall bottle stands well on the cocktail bar.

Garnier (p) Famous liqueur house in France, well known for their apricot liqueur.

Genever (g) See *Jenever*, also *Gin*.

• **Gin (g)** 40–47% Ginepro is the Italian word for juniper; Tuscany is the main source of juniper berries for use in the production of gin. Genever is one of the ways in which the Dutch say juniper, and it was in Leyden (Leiden), at the medical faculty of the university, that Dr Franciscus (or Francisco, or Sylvius) de la Boe first formulated a therapeutic elixir by distilling with the berries in the mid-1500s. Then again, maybe gin comes from the French genièvre for juniper, since it was probably in some sort of patois that the Dutch and English exchanged unpleasantries as they fought for control of the North Sea. Gin is juniper. It is an abbreviation; whether it is a corruption is a matter of debate. Before man knew how to make a pure, clean-tasting spirit, he used a variety of flavourings to enhance his impure distillates, and juniper has proven to be the most durable of them all. It has been used to impart a character and aroma to spirit, and even to beer, and among distillers it achieved the position of acceptance, and for a time indispensability, attained by the hop in the brewing business. There are many varieties of flavoured spirit, but only those made with juniper are gin, and it might be argued that even they properly qualify only if the spirit is redistilled with the magical berry. See *London Dry gin, Old Tom,*

Plymouth gin, Jenever (also known as Genever, Geneva, Hollands, Schiedam), *Steinhäger* (generically known as *Wacholder*), *Borovička*.

Grain whisky, whiskey (g) In Scotland, a continuous still product made from maize and barley, and used for the purpose of blending (see *Blended whisky*). Scottish grain whisky is not distilled to the point of neutrality, and is aged for four years. There is one Scottish grain whisky available straight, Cameron Brig. Though most American whiskey is produced from maize (corn), the distillers also use this grain to produce neutral spirit for the purpose of blending. Some of this is aged and bottled as grain whisky.

Gueuze, various spellings (g) Highly unusual vinous wheat-beer traditionally brewed in the Bruegel country near Brussels. As in traditional wine-making, fermentation is promoted by such micro-organisms as are naturally present, without the addition of yeast as an ingredient. A gueuze beer is produced to various palates and strengths by the blending and ageing of several basic brews, which are known as *Lambic* (or *Lambiek*). In a yet more unusual variation, bitter cherries are added for a second period of fermentation to produce a quenching summer beer known as *Kriek*.

Glayva (p) Approx 40% A Scottish, whisky-based liqueur flavoured with honey and herbs.

Glenfiddich (p) 40% Internationally, the best-known brand of straight (or "single") malt scotch whisky. Made by William Grant, of Glenfiddich, in the Dufftown district of Speyside (see entry below). Glenfiddich is a fine whisky, with a typically Highland combination of surprising smoothness, firm but quiet peatiness, and a fruity maturity. See *Highland malt whisky, single malt* and *Scotch whisky*.

Glenlivet (g) The proudest name in scotch whisky. deriving from a tiny distilling district. The biggest malt whisky region of Scotland is the Highlands; the most typically Highland whiskies are produced in the east; the great concentration of eastern distilleries is on Speyside (the river bisects the slice of country between Aberdeen and Inverness); and the most famous whiskies of Speyside are those in the Glenlivet style. The designation refers to the valley of a burn called the Livet, which runs into a tributory of the Spey. The fame of Glenlivet was established by the product of the first distillery to be licensed there, in 1824, that of George Smith. After a court judgment sought in 1880, this firm is the only one entitled to call its whisky simply The Glenlivet. In his excellent work *The Whiskies of Scotland*, R. J. S. McDowall describes The Glenlivet as having, "a deep mellowness and a ripe fullness of flavour, together with a delicacy of aroma which is easy to recognize". It could be argued that the only other distillery which is really in the same glen is Tamnavoulin, but the court judgment did allow the use of the district purely as a suffix to indicate a style of whisky. Several distillers use the designation, and others make whiskies in the Glenlivet style without considering it necessary to say so. Especially well-regarded examples include the flavoursome Glenfarclas, the full, smooth Macallan, and the lighter and very smooth Glen Grant, especially when it is eight years old or more (it can be found up to 25 years old). See *Highland malt whisky*, *Single malt* and *Scotch whisky*.

Golden rum (g) 40% Term commonly applied to *Rum* of that colour from Cuba, Puerto Rico and the Virgin Islands. Golden rum has a more pronounced taste and more character than its "white" brother, though both are of the light-bodied type. The colour derives from caramel, and the rum is aged for a minimum of three years.

Goldwasser (g) See *Danziger Goldwasser*.

• **Grand Marnier (p)** 35–40% A cognac-based orange liqueur of the highest quality, made by a respected French liqueur house. The fruit is of the *Curaçao* type, and it is steeped in the brandy. The yellow riband version is of a lower strength.

Grappa (g) 40%+ A coarse, country spirit that features in Hemingway novels. Grappa is the name used in Italy and California for a brandy distilled from the skins, pips and stalks of grapes, sometimes known as the pomace. Some grappa is distilled in a pot still, some by a method in which steam is forced through the pomace in vessels rather like pressure cookers. Young grappa is very fiery, but it mellows a little with age, and is sometimes matured in wood. Its character is very dry and woody, and inspires both a devoted following and a deal of scorn. A sometimes finer version is made in France, where it is called *Marc*. The same type of spirit is made in Spain as *Aguardiente*, in Portugal as bagaceira, in Germany as tresterschnapps, and under a variety of names in other countries.

Grenadine (g) A sweet syrup flavoured with pomegranate juice, containing little or no alcohol.

Gyokuro (g) Tea used in Japanese liqueur.

Haitian rum (g) 40%— Medium-bodied *Rum* of excellent quality, twice distilled in a pot still. Made from cane juice rather than molasses.

Heering, Cherry or Peter (p) 25% Respected label of dryish cherry liqueur produced in Copenhagen. See *Cherry brandy*.

Hefe German word for yeast. In labelling, indicates a high-quality sedimented beer or a humble type of brandy made from lees, the yeasty fallout of wine production.

Heublein Major American liqueur company, with Smirnoff as its best-known product.

Highland malt whisky (g) 40–60% Has the smoothest and most subtle palate of the four malt whisky styles. (See also *Lowland*, *Islay* and *Campbeltown*). There are 60-odd highland malt distilleries, most of them north of an imaginary line which runs from Greenock to Dundee. The lion's share of their output goes into blends (see *Malt* and *Scotch whisky*). The number of *Single malts* on the market at any one time varies, since a distillery which normally sells all of its output for blending may occasionally decide to make a bottling of a particularly good batch. Some single malts may appear in more than one guise, since the same whisky may be marketed by a distillery, a bottling or bonding company, a merchant, or an individual shop. A distillery may also market its product at several different ages and strengths. The highland malt style is typified by the products of the Glenlivet and Dufftown areas on Speyside (see *Glenlivet* and *Glenfiddich*); those farther north have more variation in character, and those from the islands of the north, while being classified as highland malts, often resemble their cousins from Islay. Notable malts from the far north include the atypically fragrant Glenmorangie, the dry and flavoursome Balblair, the very highly flavoured Clynelish, and the magnificent peaty Highland Park, from the Orkneys.

Hock (g) Imprecise English term for the white wines of the Rhine, and pedantically those of the Rheingau region since the word is an Anglicized abbreviation of Hochheim, a wine-producing town near Wiesbaden. Though Hochheim's wines are of a very high quality, the best-known vineyards of the Rheingau are farther down river at Johannisberg. The Rheingau produces superb wines from the German Riesling grape, flowery and spicy, with a delicate balance between acidity and sweetness, and growing richer with age. Hock is traditionally served in a glass with a thick, knobbly, tinted stem. The other wine-producing regions of Germany are Rhine-Hesse, Middle Rhine, Rhineland Palatinate (Pfalz), Moselle-Saar-Ruhr, Middle Moselle, Ahr, Nahe, Baden, Württemberg, and Franconia.

Hollands From the Dutchman's adjective to describe the products of his own country, this word passed into the English language as a description for gin when the juniper spirit arrived from The Netherlands. See *Jenever*.

Infusion In the production of liqueurs, the steeping of fruit in water in order to extract flavour.

Irish Mist (p) 40% Liqueur produced in the old distilling town of Tullamore, from Irish whiskey and heather honey. Said to be based on a recipe taken to continental Europe by Irish refugees fleeing from the Tudor armies of England.

Irish whiskey (g) 40%+ That coffee confection may have done much to popularize the Hibernian spirit in a heathen world, but this has proven to be a mixed blessing, obscuring the true position of Irish as one of the world's great drinks. The Irish have the world's oldest distillery, and they were probably the first people to make whiskey. It seems likely that they knew how to distil from grain in early medieval times, and that Irish monks took the skill to Scotland—as missionaries, of course. Although the two countries' national spirits today are much more closely related to each other than to their American cousins, they none the less differ very substantially. Perhaps the most surprising of the differences concerns the means by which the malt is kilned. Ireland, of all countries, might be expected to use peat, but it doesn't. The Irish use coal, which does not influence the taste, and the Scots use the peat, which does. In the matter of raw materials, Irish is unique among serious whiskies in that, as well as barley, an uncooked cereal is used. This is usually unmalted barley, though small proportions of wheat, rye and, notably, oats have variously been employed. A further unique feature of the traditional Irish method is the use of a triple distillation process. This method employs the pot still, to which the Irish long maintained an exclusive loyalty. The pot stills used in Ireland are larger than those favoured by the Scots, and of a slightly different design. The type of mash used gives Irish a full barley flavour which is not offset by the peaty smokiness of scotch, but the degree of rectification in the triple-distilling process balances this by having a lightening effect and creating a notable cleanness of palate. Until comparatively recently, most Irish was straight pot still whiskey, but the majority of brands are now blended with grain. In general, Irish whiskeys are aged more than those made across the water, though the Scots mature for considerably longer than the three years required by law. Like the Scots, the Irish age in sherry casks, though they also use bourbon or rum casks, and sometimes new American oak. The Irish have been moving away from their traditional medium-heavy style towards a lighter whiskey. It is to be hoped that they do not take this moderation to extremes. It would be not only Ireland's loss but also the world's if Hibernia settled for a bastard version of scotch in order to meet an international taste for the light, the bland and the innocuous. What Irish drinkers order as "a ball of malt" has much to commend it to the palates of the growing numbers of drinkers who seek flavour, character and authenticity. Although there are now only three whiskey distilleries in Ireland, and all owned by the one company, each of their brands is consciously different. One distillery is in County Cork, at Midleton, and the other two are in County Antrim, at Coleraine and Bushmills. The latter, licensed in 1608, is said with some confidence to be the oldest distillery in the world. Bushmills Black Label, a very malty blend, is one of the most fully flavoured whiskeys in Ireland. Crested Ten and Jameson 15-year-old are excellent pot still whiskeys. Power's Gold Label is the biggest seller in Ireland.

Island malt whisky (g) 40–50% There is in Scotland one island that is understandably proud that its whiskies are recognized as a style in their own right. That island is Islay, in the south-west (see below). Its whiskies are known simply as Islay malts. Some enthusiasts argue that those other islands that distil are at least jointly worthy of a classification to distinguish their whiskies, usually rather peaty in character, from the mainland's malts. If there were to be a recognized category known as the island malts, it would include those of Scapa and Highland Park, in the Orkneys; the very highly regarded Talisker, from Skye; and the aromatic but relatively light Jura Pure Malt.

Islay malt whisky (g) 40–46% Pronounced eye-la. A beautiful island, thickly covered in peat, which produces whiskies so strongly flavoured and so dry that they are said to have the iodine tang of seaweed. Held in awe by connoisseurs, usually hated by first-time drinkers, the whiskies of Islay are an essential component of most blended scotches. The classic Islay Malt in single form is Laphroaig, though Lagavulin deserves attention as an extraordinarily dry whisky, and all of the island's products are rich in flavour, bouquet and character.

Izarra (p) 50% green, 40% yellow The liqueur of the Basque country, made on the French side of the frontier, flavoured with plants from the Pyrenees, and based on armagnac. Izarra is the Basque word for star. Although the original is an old-established patent recipe, its makers now use the name as a brand on their range of liqueurs. A frappé made with Izarra itself in equal proportion to armagnac is known as a Green Beret Basque. With its bouquet of mimosa honey, the liqueur is also a most agreeable addition to desserts and jellies.

Jack Daniel's (p) 45% A famous and very fine brand of American whiskey, made in Tennessee with painstaking care, and mellowed by a thorough and elaborate process of filtration through sugar-maple charcoal. Although much is made of the flavour and fragrance said to be imparted by the *Sour Mash* process, this is quite commonly used in the production of American whiskeys. Jack Daniel's has become an element of Americana not only for its quality and its distinctive square-sided bottle, but also for its history. Dating back to 1866, Jack Daniel's is the oldest registered distillery in the United States, and the company has done much to preserve the contemporary appearance of its tiny home-town, Lynchburg (population 361). Despite its pride in Tennessee, Jack Daniel's is a whiskey of the bourbon type. The same is true of the brand's excellent rival, George Dickel Tennessee sour mash, which is also filtered through sugar-maple charcoal.

• **Jamaica rum (g)** 40–75% In its traditional form, the most rich, buttery full-bodied and pungent of the rums, in the manner of the old British Caribbean. Jamaica rums are still often shipped to England for oak ageing and blending in bonded warehouses at ports like London and Liverpool. Hence the expression London dock rum. The most traditional of Jamaica rums are double-distilled in pot stills, and their special character derives from the re-incorporation of residues from various stages of production. The residue from the distillation itself, known as dunder, is fermented and then reused to promote a natural fermentation. This is the most elaborate such process in the production of alcoholic drinks, but it is to some extent reminiscent of the sour mash in whisky production and of various techniques used in the brewing of especially characterful beers. Perhaps the rather old-fashioned English insult "dunderhead" was originally aimed at someone whose mind appeared to have been dulled by rummy excess. A heavy rum made by the dunder process is known in Jamaica as a Plummer type (g), and an even heavier one as a Wedderburn (g). See *Rum*.

Jenever (Genever, Geneva, etc.) (g) 35–40% Gin, in its original and unabbreviated form (see *Gin* for derivation). Also sometimes known as Hollands, or as Schiedam, from the name of the traditional distilling town, near Rotterdam. Today, the biggest distillery is nearer to Amsterdam, and the style of gin commonly used throughout the world is London Dry. As the more recent distillers, the English quickly adopted the technology to make a highly purified base spirit, and this highlights the flowery dryness imparted by the botanical flavourings; the Dutch, as in earlier times, persist with a less "pure" spirit that retains some of the flavours of its grainy base. This is produced from equal parts of rye, barley and maize by a double distillation process in a pot still. The resultant "malt wine" is then blended, according to the palate required, with a neutral spirit that has been redistilled with the botanical flavourings characteristically used in gin. Juniper is by definition the dominant botanical flavouring in all types of gin, and coriander is among the ingredients used in both English and Dutch types, but in The Netherlands caraway and aniseed are also significant. Unlike English gin, the Dutch type is aged, but young (jonge) and old (oude) variations differ more in style than maturity. Young jenever, which is the more popular in The Netherlands, is very lightly flavoured, and can have a disappointing lack of character, though this varies from brand to brand. *Bols* produce a very neutral young jenever under their own name, but their Claeryn label has a jonge with an interesting balance of juniper and "malt wine". Old jenevers have a pronounced "malt wine" taste. The initials Z.O., from the Dutch words meaning very old, have no precise meaning. Since production of jenever predates the division of the Low Countries into two kingdoms, a spirit of the same type is also produced in Belgium. The centre for distillation there is the town of Hasselt, in Belgian Limburg, though the city of Ghent is known for its partiality to jenever. In both countries, there are tiny private distillers whose products are well worth trying. There are also fruit-flavoured jenevers. The Dutch and Belgians drink their jenever straight up, very cold, in small tulip-shaped glasses, as an apéritif or a hard liquor, and it is commonly held that continental gins are not suitable for use with mixers because of their very pronounced taste. This is a debatable proposition. Young jenevers are not strongly flavoured, and it is arguable whether Dutch gins are as aromatic as they are said to be. Cocktails are made successfully with rye and bourbon, which have a considerably fuller flavour.

Jerez Too difficult for the English to pronounce with the proper lisp, so the Castilian "Hereth" is "*Sherry*" elsewhere. The town of Jerez is the capital of the sherry-producing country, which runs between Cadiz and Seville, in Andalusia, the most southerly region of Spain. The English may have developed a taste for stolen sherry during the sacking of Spanish ports in the sixteenth century. Later, merchants from the British Isles established themselves in Jerez, and English ports like London and Bristol found their way on to sherry labels.

Kabänes (p) Approx 35% The liqueur of Cologne, a patent semi-bitter recipe of excellent quality, available outside its homeland in cities with large German communities, like Chicago.

•**Kahlua (p)** 26.5% Coffee liqueur originating from Mexico and very popular in the United States. Taken as an after-dinner drink, used in desserts, and employed in many mixed drinks.

•**Kirsch, Kirschwasser (g)** 45% The most famous of the fruit brandies made in the area where France, Germany and Switzerland meet (see *Eau-de-vie*). Kirsch is the French-language name. *Wasser* is added in the German-language version to indicate a spirit distilled from the fermented fruit. If the fruit is first macerated in alcohol, which is then redistilled, the suffix becomes -geist. The French distil.at a sufficiently low point to retain the flavour of the fruit, while the Germans aim for a drier, stronger spirit. Kirschwasser, a strong, dry, cherry distillate, is especially renowned when made in the Black Forest. It is used deliciously to moisten the Schwarzwalder torte, the typical gâteau of the Forest.

Klarer (g) Generic term used in Germany for clear corn *Schnapps* or *Steinhäger* gin.

Kölsch (g) The German word meaning "from Cologne", especially applied to an unusual pale, brass-coloured top-fermented beer unique to the city and its environs and popular there as both an apéritif and a digestif. Very well suited to the latter role because of its alkaline composition. A common local snack is a glass of kölsch (4.5) with "half a hen", which turns out to be a wedge of cheese, or "Cologne caviare", which is a type of blutwurst.

Korn (g) Approx 35% Clear grain spirit drunk in northern Germany, often with a beer chaser. Korn, which originates from the Harz mountains, is usually distilled in a pot still, and sometimes aged.

Kriek (g) 5–7% Cherry beer of excellent quality which is traditionally a summer drink in the Brussels area.
See *Gueuze*.

Krupnik (g) 35–40% A sometimes coarse honey vodka made in the Slavic countries.

Kümmel (g) 35–45% A peripatetic liqueur made with caraway, cumin seeds, fennel, orris and other herbs. In the beginning, as now, kümmel was made by *Bols* in Amsterdam. It is said to have been developed by the pioneer distiller Lucas Bols in the late sixteenth century. The drink is then reported to have been enjoyed by Peter the Great in extraordinary circumstances. He was apparently working incognito as a labourer in The Netherlands, learning shipbuilding techniques with a view to starting a Russian navy. He took kümmel east, the story goes, and it subsequently reappeared as a rather sweeter liqueur some centuries later in a distillery at Allasch Castle, near Riga, Latvia, bearing the label of Mentzendorff. Political upheavals took that particular recipe variously to Germany and, by some homing instinct, to the Low Countries. Similar travails affected the house of Wolf-schmidt, which elevated kümmel to a crystalline majesty and a strength of 60%. Even the dry Berlin-style kümmel is now made in Hamburg, where the Gilka label is properly held in very high regard. Such has been the determination of liqueurists to safeguard their kümmel recipes wherever they were obliged to travel. Their journeys make light of those experienced by the men of maraschino, the monks of Chartreuse, the house of Zwack, to name but a few.

Kvass, quass (g) Coarse Russian "beer" made from rye bread and, unaccountably, sometimes emulated by home-brewers in the United States. The technique is, though, worthy of a certain veneration, since it dates back to Ancient Egypt.

Lambic, lambiek (g) Vinous wheat-beer made near Brussels. Still and cider-like, an acquired taste, but with a devoted following. Commonly used in blending. See *Gueuze*.

• **Lager (g)** From the German word to store. An omnibus term for any bottom-fermented beer, whether its style is derived from Pilsen (or even Budweis) in Bohemia, Munich in Bavaria, Vienna, Dortmund or Einbeck ("*Bock*"). An overwhelming majority of the world's beers are made by bottom-fermentation whether their labels say so or not. Beers made in this way should be stored for some weeks by the brewer so that they mature before being sold, hence the name. Bottom and top refer to the position of the yeast as it settles in the fermentation tank. The technique of bottom-fermentation came into widespread use in the mid and late 1800s after Pasteur had helped both brewers and wine-makers to understand fully for the first time how yeasts performed. Bottom-fermentation offered beers of more stability, consistency and sparkle than had previously been achieved with top-fermentation (the method still used to produce ale and stout). The older method, however, is held by connoisseurs to produce beers of more flavour and character. In this sense, there is an analogy with the pot and patent methods of distillation.

Leroux (p) Major American liqueur company.

• **Light rum (g)** 40% Refers to lightness of body, rather than colour. A light rum may be colourless ("white" or "silver"), or it may be aged for three years or more, in which case it will have more flavour, and then be coloured with caramel ("amber" or "gold"). The lightness of body is achieved by distillation initially to a high alcoholic content, in continuous stills. Like most spirits, the rum is diluted to the required strength for marketing. Light-bodied rums are the style of the Spanish-speaking Caribbean, and especially Cuba, Puerto Rico and the Virgin Islands.

Light whisky, whiskey Term most commonly used in the United States, and reflecting a fear of flavour. The lightness is in body rather than colour, though the two are sometimes mistakenly perceived as being directly related. The body of a scotch whisky can be diminished if it is blended from a high proportion of grain, or if notably light malts are used. American light whiskeys are the product of distillation to a higher alcoholic content than is normal, followed by a greater degree of dilution. By being more thoroughly distilled than a regular American whiskey, they lose body. They are aged in uncharred casks.

Lillet (p) 17% Only the practised will publicly try the trick of squeezing the zest of lemon and flaming the spray over the drink with a match, but even a virgin Lillet is an apéritif of elegance and individuality. This French patent vermouth is among the lighter and drier of its type, with an orangey tinge. The most common version has a full white-wine colour, but there is also a sweeter red Lillet.

Linie Aquavit See *Aquavit*.

Liqueur (g) To the French, any after-dinner drink, as in liqueur brandy. To the British, specifically a sweetish drink created from a ready-made spirit base into which is infused, macerated or re-distilled flavouring agents such as roots, barks, flowers, fruits or seeds. The term liqueur is also used in the United States, though American counterparts are often referred to, confusingly, as cordials. In Britain, a *Cordial* is a flavoured syrup with little or no alcoholic content.

London dock rum See *Jamaica rum*.

London Dry gin (g) 40–47% Having come from The Netherlands (see *Gin*), juniper elixir was made more or less in the Dutch way (see *Jenever*) for two centuries. When William of Orange came from The Netherlands to rule over England with his consort Mary, one of the regime's first acts was to ban the import of French brandies, and grant every citizen the right to distil, both measures helping farmers find outlets for their grain. The flood of amateurish gin which ensued was still in full spate when the people of Britain had to be anaesthetized through the change from a rural life to that of the world's first industrialized and urban nation. It was then that gin became synonymous with exploitation and misery, and perhaps that is why distillers seized the chance to produce a spirit of greater rectitude when the technology became available with the introduction of the patent still from the 1830s onwards. While the Dutch stuck to their full-bodied gins, retaining the flavour of the grain, the English used the patent still to produce a neutral spirit base. Perhaps that removed the need for heavy, sweet flavourings, giving rise to the dry gins which became popular in London in the 1870s. The base spirit for London Dry gin may be distilled from grain or from some other raw material such as molasses, but it has been rectified to neutrality before it is then redistilled with the botanical flavourings in a pot still. While juniper is the essential ingredient of all gins, and coriander is common to both Dutch and English, there are certain additional botanicals which are especially favoured by the London distillers, though each label has its own particular formula. The most significant botanicals used in the various London recipes are angelica root, cassia and cinnamon bark, orange peel, lemon peel and almonds. London Dry established itself in good time for the Cocktail Age. Since whiskies and brandies have a much fuller body, and flavourless vodka was then unknown in the West, the neutral background of London Dry gin made it the most suitable base for cocktails. Furthermore, its botanical flavourings match or complement those used in vermouth and in many of the liqueurs that are used in cocktails. As distillers elsewhere took up dry gin, it became accepted that London indicated the style rather than the place of production. Though none is better than that produced in England, dozens of countries make their own "London" dry gin, of greatly varying quality. Ireland has a Cork dry gin, and Minorca has its own distinctive variation on the theme. See *Plymouth gin, Sloe gin.*

Lovage (p) Herbal alcoholic cordial of low strength drunk as a digestif, added to brandy, port or rum, or used as a hangover cure in the west of England.

Lowland malt whisky (g) 40%+ The sweet, light and feathery Rosebank (p) is a fine embodiment of lowland malt whisky, but this category is sadly unsung. One reason is that few lowland malts go straight into the bottle; another is that a good few of the distilleries are in unpicturesque industrial locations.

Maceration The steeping of fruit in alcohol in the production of liqueurs. This process may take as long as a year.

Madeira (g) 15–20% Fortified wine from the island of the same name, in the Atlantic off the coast of Morocco. In addition to being fortified with brandy, madeira is heated for four or five months at a temperature of 120°F or more. While the original wine of the island is acidic and unpleasant, this process produces a distinctive drink of great character, with a caramel tang. There are four types: sercial is drunk as an aperitif, and resembles a fuller fino sherry; verdelho has a tinge of honey and a smoky taste, is drunk either as an aperitif or a digestif; bual is a dessert wine; the dark, fragrant, soft malmsey is a famous after-dinner drink and weapon of the seducer. Although the island of Madeira is historically linked with Portugal, its wines were once in every well-found English home (see also *Port*), and were also popular in the United States. They remain important in French cuisine, and are extremely popular in northern Europe.

Málaga (g) Fortified wine from the ancient town of Málaga, on the south coast of Spain. Made by a complicated process involving the use of grape musts and dried grapes. Dark, sweet, and once fashionable, but now rarely seen outside of Spain and Latin America.

Malmsey See *Madeira*.

Malt whisky, whiskey (g) In Scotland, a whisky made in a pot still exclusively from malted barley. In the United States, a whiskey made in a continuous still or pot still from not less than 51 per cent malted barley. See **Scotch.**

Malvasia The grape used to produce malmsey, and rich brown wines elsewhere in the world.

Mandarine Napoléon (p) 40% Elegant proprietary liqueur. Napoleon is said to have wooed his favourite actress with a similar citrus potion, and Francophiles in Belgium took up the theme. Confusingly, the French language describes as a mandarine what English deems to be a tangerine, and it is from this fruit that the liqueur is made. The fruits of Tangier are in this instance Andalusian. They are macerated in aged cognac by the respected liqueurist Alfred Fourcroy.

Manzanilla (g) A most unusual once-removed *Sherry* of excellent quality but highly individualistic palate. Not from *Jerez*, but from nearby Sanlúcar de Barrameda. Manzanilla is so extraordinarily dry that some people find it almost bitter, and it has a notably delicate bouquet. These two characteristics are said to be imparted by the salty sea air. An excellent apéritif.

• **Maraschino (g)** 30%– Distinctive type of cherry liqueur originating from Dalmatia, though the most famous marques are now made in Italy. Extensively used in cocktails. See *Cherry brandy*.

Marc (g) 40–45% The French name for grape skins, and for the brandy that is made from them, the counterpart of grappa, tresterschnapps and others. Marc is said to be much more delicate than its cousins, but it still inspires derision and devotion in equal proportions. Even outside France the marcs of Burgundy enjoy some reputation, and among them the brandyman Cyril Ray draws attention to Meursault. He also notes the marcs of Champagne and Alsace, in the latter case especially the Gewürtztraminer. A Burgundian cheese soaked in the spirit is known as époisses confit au marc. This is not to be confused with tomme au marc de raisin, which is merely coated with grape pulp and pips for strong teeth and stomachs.

Marie Brizard (p) Famous French liqueur house noted for its *Anisette*, and for its *Apricot brandy*. The lady who founded the firm in the 1700s is said to have been inspired by a recipe she received as a gift from a West Indian whom she successfully nursed through an illness.

Marsala (g) 15–18% Like so many fortified wines, marsala was created with the aid of the British. In this case, a Liverpool merchant settled in the Sicilian port of Marsala, and supplied Nelson's fleet with wine from there. The marsala process employs heated grape juice, and the end product has a burnt-sugar palate. One fairly dry marsala none the less offers itself as an aperitif, while lovers of sweet, dark wines find the more typical treacly style quite delicious. A sort of marsala liqueur is made with egg yolk and other flavourings, and the wine is an ingredient of the classic Italian dessert zabaglione. A bar can exist without marsala, but a kitchen cannot.

Martini and Rossi (p) Famous *Vermouth* producers with headquarters near Turin. Despite its size and international organization, Martini and Rossi is still a family firm. Signor Rossi gave his name to an aperitif bitters made by the firm, and Signor Martini to the famous range of vermouths. Although the dry one is often used to effect in the cocktail of the same name, this is coincidental. The cocktail was invented by a barman called Martini, in New York, and French vermouth was originally used. See *Dry Martini* (page 109).

Martinique rum (g) 40%+ At its best, very much the *Rum* (or rhum) of the French Caribbean. Full-bodied and pungent, made from cane juice rather than molasses, and distilled in a pot still. In some cases, the dunder process (see *Jamaica rum*) is used.

Mastika, various spellings (g) 40%+ Brandy-based anis or liquorice liqueur resinated with the gum of the mastic bush. Made in the Balkans, Greece and Cyprus.

Médoc (g) Not only the wine from that district of Bordeaux but also a liqueur, Cordial Médoc (p) 40%. A curious concoction of flavours and herbs on a base of local wine.

Metaxa (p) 42% Fully flavoured and aromatic brandy from the firm of the same name, Greece's biggest distillers. The grapes are usually from Attica. Greek brandy is sometimes rather sweet and sticky. It may even be further sweetened so that it qualifies as a liqueur, though to what purpose is not quite clear. The best of Greek brandies are quite agreeable, especially after a feast of kleftiko or bastourma.

Menthe, crème de (g) 25–30% Sweet liqueur flavoured with various types of mint. The green version looks more interesting, but the "white" is exactly the same. Crème de menthe frappé is a refreshing and palate-clearing digestif, and the liqueur is extensively used in cocktails. Highly regarded brands include Freezomint (p) and the oddly named Pippermint Get (p).

Mezcal (g) 35–45%+ The machismo spirit of Mexico, for anyone who fancies tripping South of the Border. The mezcal is a plant of the genus agave or maguey. There are those who think its distilled juice tastes like old zapatos, though it could more forcefully be argued that some of the brands exported from the town of *Tequila* are unduly refined. No, it's not made from cactus.

Milk Sherry (g) British term for a smooth, sweet *Sherry* based on an Oloroso. No precise meaning, nor any precise distinction between "milk" and "cream" sherries.

Milk Stout (g) Colloquial British term for a faintly lactic sweet *Stout* of low alcoholic content. Mackeson (p) is the classic example.

Mirabelle (g) 45% Fine "white" brandy of the *Eau-de-vie* type distilled from the yellow Mirabelle plum in France, Germany and Switzerland.

Mistelle (g) A mixture of surplus brandy and fresh grape juice of the same locality. The word mistelle may be used colloquially to describe this blend when it has been aged to produce a sweetish but substantial apéritif known as *Ratafia* (especially in the Champagne area) or *Pineau* (especially in the Charentes). Or it may be used in a more technical sense to describe the mixture as one of the components of a French *Vermouth*.

Montilla (g) 16% Delicate wine of great distinction which is a first cousin of *Sherry*, though it is not fortified. Made in Andalusia, but inland, near Cordoba, where the hot climate provides grapes with a high sugar content for rapid fermentation. This is carried out in clay jars of an Eastern appearance, a reminder that Cordoba was the capital of Moorish Spain. Montilla is a delightfully Spanish apéritif. In the *World Atlas of Wine*, Hugh Johnson says of these wines: "People claim to find in them the scent of black olives (which are, of course, their perfect partners)."

Moscatel (g) Sweet wine made from the muscat or moscato grape, different varieties of which grow throughout southern Europe and the Mediterranean. A particularly fine, scenty moscatel is made in Setubal, Portugal. The same grape family is used to produce sparkling wines in Italy and California. The fruity wine called muscadet is made from a quite different grape.

Mow Toy (g) 45% Malodorous grain spirit made in Hong Kong.

Münchener (g) 4% – Term used in many countries for a malty, dark *Lager* beer of the type made famous by Munich brewers in the 1800s. In Germany today, these brews are identified as being *dunkel* (dark), to distinguish them from the *hell* (light) style of malty beer subsequently popularized by the Münchener brewers.

Muscatelle, muscadelle Variations on *Moscatel*. See above.

"Napoléon" brandy Boney is often invoked to describe a *Cognac* which is at least five years old. Oddly, the Napoléon brandy of a particular house is apt to be its second best rather than its very best. Courvoisier claim that their brandy was laid aside for Napoléon when, after his abdication, he planned to leave secretly for the United States. They use "the brandy of Napoléon" as a slogan of the house. Occasionally, auction rooms have sold for substantial sums brandies alleged to date back to the time of Napoléon. No one has ever been able to authenticate the age of these brandies, and there is scant likelihood of their having been around at the time of Napoléon. While a brandy of such age would no doubt be of great historical interest, it would be no more mature today than when it was bottled. In glass, brandy does not improve, and in the cask it deteriorates after about 70 years. See also *Mandarine Napoléon*.

New England rum (g) No longer a recognized category. *Rum* was the first spirit distilled in North America, and the industry in New England was the banker of the triangular trade. Some of the rum was taken to Africa and exchanged for slaves, who were then taken to the Caribbean and traded for molasses, which was brought back to New England as a raw material.

Nocino (g) Approx 30% A delicious, bitter Italian digestif made from nuts, with a forgiving hint of sweetness in the aftertaste.

Noilly Prat (p) 17% The best-known French dry vermouth, made in Marseilles. Very dry. Excellent in a dry Martini cocktail, or as an apéritif with lots of ice and just a little soda. Made with two white wines and 40 herbs, steeped for a year and a half. In Britain, where "French" was once a familiar term for dry vermouth, a famous slogan punningly proposed, "say Noilly Prat and your French is perfect".

Noyau, crème de Sometimes *Noyaux* **(g)** 25–30% Almond-flavoured liqueur made from the kernels of peaches, apricots or other stone fruits. A rather sweet digestif, also useful in cocktails. Colourless and pink versions, of which the finest is made by the French firm of Veuve Champion.

Okolehao, Oke (g) A Hawaian spirit made from sugar and rice, and flavoured with a local root.

Old Tom gin (p) A very old brand of sweetened London gin.

Oloroso (g) The third principal class of *Sherry*, dark and sweet. A dessert wine, or the basis of a good-quality sweet sherry.

Orange bitters (g) 15%+ A very dry essence that is a traditional and valued ingredient in cocktails.

Not always easy to find in retail liquor stores, but worth seeking out. Major liqueur houses and gin distillers still make orange bitters.

- **Orange-flower water (g)** Light non-alcoholic essence originating from France that is used to great effect in some cocktails, notably the Ramos Fizz of New Orleans.

Orange liqueurs The most famous are the *Curaçao* family, made from the peel of the small green oranges native to the island of that name in the former Dutch West Indies (Netherlands Antilles). Among the different degrees of dryness in curaçao, triple sec has become almost a liqueur in its own right, as has its original and most famous producer, the firm of *Cointreau*. Dutch and German distillers make Half and Half (g) liqueurs which are a mix of curaçao and various spices and there are many other variations. Another Dutch creation is a citrus and herb liqueur called Pimpeltjens (p), made by De Kuyper. South Africa has a liqueur called *Van der Hum* (g) based on a local variety of tangerine, Italy the excellent brandy-based herbal orange liqueur called *Aurum*, Belgium its elegant *Mandarine Napoléon*, and there are many more proprietary brands elsewhere in the world.

Orgeat (g) A non-alcoholic almond flavoured syrup used in cocktails.

Ouzo Sometimes *Douzico* (g) 40% Well-known and popular *Absinthe* substitute from Greece. When diluted with ice and water as is customary with such drinks, ouzo turns white rather than the greeny-yellow of its French cousins. It is also drier than they are.

Parfait Amour (g) 30% Perfect love is, it seems, a sweet and sickly experience which is not particularly constant. Though most major liqueur producers, in Europe at least, make perfect love, there seems little agreement about the way in which this is done. Liqueurist Peter Hallgarten reckons it is something like crème de *Violettes*, with additional flavour from flower petals, and a sweet citrus base. Perfect love is, he says, scented and slightly spicy. There are those who would argue specifically for orange, flower of cinnamon and peach stones.

Pastis (g) 45% From the French word for mixture, a pastiche of ingredients that provides a more liquorice-tasting alternative to *Pernod*. Pastis has a brownish tinge when neat and is paler than Pernod when diluted. There are a number of brands, among which Ricard is the best known. Pastis are especially popular in Provence. Ready-mixed and flavoured variations are also marketed. See *Absinthe*.

Pasha (p) 25%+ Coffee liqueur from Turkey.

Peach A reticent but versatile performer at the cocktail bar. Peach bitters are as hard to find as their orangey cousins, and every bit as worthwhile. Persico and variations are distilled from peach leaves, and are still to be found in liqueur capitals like Amsterdam and Paris. The French call peach liqueurs Pèche, and other countries have their own versions. The delicious fruit is the most pronounced flavour in *Southern Comfort*.

Peppermint Schnapps 20–30% Increasingly popular in the United States as a much less sweet and lighter-bodied substitute for crème de *Menthe*. Schnapps not for its potency but for its base, which is a pot still spirit in the German style.

Peppers In some countries, hot and spicy liqueurs are made from peppers. The best-known example is a traditional spicy vodka from Russia called Okhotnichya (g) 38.5%, in which peppers are a dominant flavouring among several other spices, herbs and berries. A home-made version can be created if hot peppers are steeped for several weeks in plain vodka.

Percolation Process used in the manufacture of liqueurs, in which the spirit base, cold, hot or in vapour form, is passed through a container filled with the natural flavouring agents, which in this case may be herbs. This process may have to be repeated for weeks or months to achieve the desired level of extraction.

Pernod (p) 45% The original *Absinthe* substitute, and by far the most famous, though its makers are at persistent pains to proclaim the innocence and individuality of their product. Their elixir is surely safe, and over the years its popularity has remained undented by its local rivals, or such Franco-Americana as Oxygenee and Herbsaint, the latter cleverly pronouncing its antecedence. Drinks of this type are commonly diluted with four to five parts of water, over ice. In the south of France and north of Spain, more especially Provence and Catalonia, they are drunk both as aperitifs and liqueurs with great style. A bar-fitting specially for the Pernod drinker is the watercooler with tiny taps for the customer, such as is found not only in southern Europe but also in certain Francophile haunts in London and

New Orleans. Another refinement is a funnel that rests atop a glass of neat Pernod or pastis. A cube of sugar is placed over the hole in the funnel, and ice is packed on top. Water is then poured into the funnel and allowed to drip slowly through ice and sugar into the drink.

•Perrier (p) Hannibal is believed to have refreshed himself with Perrier; the Romans built baths at the spring, which is near Nîmes, in the south of France; and it was Napoleon III who decreed that the waters should be bottled and made available "for the good of France". The spring was first commercially exploited by A. W. St John Harmsworth, of the London newspaper dynasty, who bought the source as a gift to his tutor, a Dr Perrier, who was a collector of such things. Harmsworth, an enthusiast for sport and gymnastics who was later crippled in a road accident in France, suggested that the Perrier bottle be shaped like an Indian club. All of this happened long before Perrier was given the stamp of approval by New Yorkers as "the power drink", and that with the addition of lime juice. Though there are those who would argue against the use of mineral-tasting waters in mixed drinks, the edge of Perrier offsets the stickiness of fruit juices, and it does interesting things to the taste of gin. Such playful behaviour aside, Perrier more than any other mineral water can stand alone as a drink of considerable character. It has the useful attribute through its alkaline composition of being both a digestif and a speedy soother of hangovers, yet its saltiness is so slight as not to impair its quenching qualities whatever.

Persico (g) See *Peach*.

Petrus Boonekamp (p) See *Boonekamp*.

Péychaud (p) See *Bitters*.

Pilsener (g) 5% The world's best-known beer style. The original was first brewed at Pilsen, in Bohemia, now a part of Czechoslovakia, in 1842. With its golden glister, its hoppy dryness, its clean taste, and its Perrier-like digestif qualities, it became the most popular of the new bottom-fermented beers, which were the toast of German-speaking Europe. Like its counterpart in Budweis, and its contemporaries in Vienna and Munich, it was widely imitated, and its celebrity was taken to the New World in the Hungry Forties by German emigrés, later to be the founders of the modern American brewing industry. Only the original brewery is legally entitled to call its product Urquell Pilsner (p). The prefix means "the original source of". Most imitators use the spelling Pilsener. See *Lager*.

Pimento The dried aromatic berries of the Jamaica pepper tree are used to make a liqueur in the Caribbean and elsewhere in the Americas.

Pineau des Charentes (g) 17% Sweetish, bland but agreeable and substantial apéritif made in its own appellation controlée region of the Cognac country by the blending of surplus brandy with fresh grape juice in a ratio of two to one. The best Pineau is aged in wood. It is served very cold, and can be reinforced with vodka or a drying calvados. Pineau is the Charentais form of *Ratafia*. See also *Mistelle*.

Plymouth gin (g) 40% Gin came from Leiden to Plymouth, and so did the Pilgrim Fathers, on their way to the New World. Sadly for mythology, no connection has ever been made. What is established is that gin crossed the sea with fighting men, and Plymouth is historically the home of the Royal Navy. Legend decrees that it was the Navy who first mixed gin with Angostura Bitters, an elixir invented by a military doctor in the Caribbean as cure for tropical ills. Today, Pink Gin (see Mixed Drinks section, p 132) is still properly made with Plymouth gin. As a recognized and protected style of dry gin, Plymouth was traditionally heavier and more aromatic than London. Over the years, the distillers have gradually ditched distictiveness in favour of worldwide acceptability, and made their gin more like the internationally famous London version. Despite this foolish faintheartedness, they still produce a gin which is distinctively smooth, perhaps because they use natural water from Dartmoor.

Pimm's (p) 31.5% Unique form of English gin. A flavoured gin or a sling? See Mixed Drinks section, p 131.

Pisco (g) 45% Perhaps the next modish spirit, inexorable as the fashions of drinking now are. Pisco is a brandy made from muscat wine and matured for a short time in clay jars. Traditionally, it has a taste and aroma of beeswax, and is made in pot stills. Pisco is the Quechua word for bird, the name of the tribe which once made beeswax-coated amphorae in which to transport the brandy, and of the port in Peru from which it is shipped. Chile also claims to have a

71

tradition of this type of brandy, though it uses an Italian grape. The drink is also common in Bolivia. Pisco began to gain popularity in some parts of the United States in the late 1960s and early 1970s, and apopular brand is Inca (p), with its Indian-head bottle. The Pisco Punch, which is really a sour, has contributed greatly to the popularity of this once-primitive spirit.

Poire Williams, Williamine (g) 45% The bottle growing on the tree is the astonishing novelty that helps this excellent *Eau-de-vie* catch the attention of even the most unimaginative drinker. The bottle is attached to the tree so that a pear will grow inside. When both are picked, the remaining space inside the bottle is filled with a brandy made from the same fruit, the Williams pear, otherwise known as the Bartlett. Such an elaborate performance is more than a form of folk advertising; the pear in the bottle beautifully brings out the fine orchard bouquet of this blossoming brandy. The most fragrant bottle plantations are said to be in Switzerland.

Pomeranz (g) Old northern European liqueur or bitters based on unripe oranges.

Ponche (g) A "punch" liqueur from Spain, brandy based, with the flavour of sherry.

• **Port (g)** 17% Vinho do Porto, to give it its full name, which it must be accorded in some countries, including the United States, as a precaution against imitation. Port is the wine of Oporto, and the fortified wine of Portugal. Oporto is a port city in both senses of the word. It stands at the mouth of the river Douro; upstream, in rough hill country, lie the vineyards. Port wine dates from the time when the Portuguese were given trade preference by the English. The Portuguese are still described by the English as "our oldest allies", and the friendship dates back to that time. In 1703, the English were at war with France, so they took their thirst and their trade to Portugal, which agreed in return to buy British wool. The agreement, known as the Methuen Treaty after the English ambassador, overlooked the fact that Portuguese wine was hardly to the taste of people accustomed to French wines. Thus the English invented port, just as they popularized almost every other fortified wine. The wines of the Douro are fortified by the addition of local brandy, which arrests fermentation prematurely, leaving a sweetening of grape sugar in the wine. The least sweet of ports is the kind made from various white grapes. The French, today's biggest consumers of port, use the white version as an aperitif. They accord the same treatment to a run-of-the-mill red port, which is occasionally still found in an English pub as a winter drink, sometimes served in a mix with brandy or, in summer, with lemonade. Pub port is often the kind called Ruby, as if it were a barmaid, dark, rather rough, matured in wood but not for very long. A Tawny port, which should look as it sounds, and be comparatively dry, has been matured in wood for a very respectable period. It goes well with nuts at Christmas, or Stilton cheese at any available opportunity. All of these ports are blended, and aged in wood, in which habitat they mature more quickly than in the bottle. A "late-bottled vintage" or "porto of the vintage" is an unblended wine that has been aged in wood. A "vintage-character" port is intended to be laid down to mature in the bottle. As it does so, sediment will throw a "crust" on the side of the bottle. In order that the crust will not break and mix with the wine, the bottle has to be handled with great care, and decanted before the port can be served. A vintage port is an unblended wine from an exceptional year. It is not for drinking, but for keeping and bequeathing. "Eventually," promises Hugh Johnson, "perhaps after 20 years, it will have a fatness and fragrance, richness and delicacy which is incomparable." The many uses to which port is put testify to the political need of the English all those years ago to buy as much of the stuff as possible. It remains, above all, the after-dinner drink of the academic, the silk and the gentleman. Here it has yet another use to the Englishman, for it provides the litmus test of breeding. If he is a true gentleman, he will, at the dinner table, always pass the decanter clockwise.

Poteen, various spellings **(g)** The word is a diminutive for pot, and has nothing to do with praties. They may have been used from time to time, in Ireland it would be surprising if they weren't, but accounts of illicit distillation usually refer to the use of malted barley and perhaps oats. Though every spirit-drinking nation has a tradition of illicit distillation and battles with the authorities, the Irish are better story-tellers than most. There have even been a number of legitimate poteens, if that is not a contradiction in terms, but didn't the Scots produce canned Scotch mist for sale to English and American tourists? Anything goes as the song says. See *Irish Whiskey*.

Pot Still An important distinction in the production of any spirit is the type of still used, Pot or Continuous? Only the pot still is used in the production of *malt Scotch whisky* (in which beverage it is desired to retain the flavour and bouquet of both the barley and the peat) and *Cognac* (where the character of the grape and its soil survive). The pot still is used in the production of fruit *Eaux-de-vie* and dark *Jamaica rums*, and any other spirit which is intended to retain the pungency and personality of its source. This lofty aim is achieved through the stumbling, inefficient and un-thorough way in which the pot still distils. A pot still is characterful and individualistic, and so are its products. It is an old-fashioned still, with a familiar appearance, a pear-shaped "pot" (usually copper), in which the materials to be distilled are heated, and a "swan's neck" carrying their vapour to the condenser. It is a fat raconteur, which tells the stories of the materials it distils. Each distillation is a separate operation, after which it has to stop and be re-charged. If it got on with its work, if it were more efficient, it would produce a much purer distillate, which would have less flavour. That sort of work is carried out by the cost-effective, business-like, upright Patent Continuous Column Still (it is described by any of those self-explanatory adjectives, or by the name of Coffey, one of its several inventors, along with Stein and various Frenchmen). The continuous still is efficient, thorough, controllable, versatile, but lacking in idiosyncrasy. It makes grain whiskeys, light rums, and neutral spirit for vodkas and some liqueurs. In the case of *London Dry gin*, the neutral spirit base is made in a continuous still, but the botanicals are distilled in a pot still.

Prunelle French name for the sloe berry, which is made into an eau-de-vie and a liqueur in Alsace and the Loire. See *Eau-de-Vie*.

Puerto Rican rum (g) 40%+ Light-bodied, like the rums of most Spanish-speaking islands, and made in a continuous still. The best-known label is Bacardi, formerly of Cuba.

Pulque (g) The drink of the Aztecs, and still popular in Mexico. Pulque is the fermented juice or sap of the mezcal plant. When the invading Spaniards brought with them the art of distillation (newly learned from the Moors?), it became possible to convert the ferocious fermentation into a spirit, today known as mezcal unless it happens to be produced in or around the town of Tequila. See *Mezcal* and *Tequila*.

Punch Not only a spiced alcoholic, mixed drink served to a group of people from a bowl, and often containing rum, but also a bottled version of the same which has become a national drink in Sweden. See *Swedish Punsch*.

Punt e Mes (p) 17% Delicious and distinctive Milanese apéritif in the vermouth style. Very full flavour with an orangey sweetness playing against a quinine bitterness. Its rich colour merges the reddish hue of other apéritifs with more of a brown tinge, and it has a slightly syrupy consistency that is delightfully offset by a small swoosh of soda, three or four big ice cubes and a slice of lemon. In Italy, often mixed with orange juice. A particular mix gave rise to the name, a Milanese stockbroker's way of saying "a point and a half".

Quetsch (g) 45% One of the great *Eaux-de-vie*, distilled from the small, sour, bluish-purple Switzen plum.

Raki (g) 40–45% Most commonly used in Turkey, where it usually means the local *Absinthe* substitute, which is of the very dry, white type. Also used to describe any hard liquor in the Levant and points east, since it is a variation on *Arak*, Arrak, Arrack.

Ratafia (g) A word that has meant a variety of different drinks at different times and places, though always a mélange of sorts. It seems to have derived from the Creole word for rum, and perhaps it thus fell into currency during the time of French sea power. It is also said to have been used to describe a liqueur drunk at the ratification of treaties, and perhaps flavoured with nuts and fruits. A ratafia has been a flavoured version of a North African, notably Algerian, wine, and it has been also a punch-type product of the town of Grenoble. Given the geographical location of Grenoble, the latter is likely originally to have been a fruit-and-herb vermouth, which might explain today's meaning. One ingredient of a vermouth is a *Mistelle*, which is a blending of fresh grape juice with brandy. The word mistelle is also used colloquially to describe the same sort of mixture served as a drink in its own right, and that potion is known generically as ratafia, especially in the Champagne area, where it is sometimes flavoured with fruits. The same drink is made in the Charentes but there it is called *Pineau*.

Rectification The purification of spirit by redistillation. Potash salts are also added for this purpose.

Retsina The unmistakable wine of Greece, with a powerfully resinous palate which many a drinker shrinks from at first taste but grows to love. About half the wine produced in Greece is resinated, notably that grown in Attica, the region of Athens, and it is available in both white and rosé versions. It is not a Balkan drink but a Greek one, and apparently has been since ancient times. Hugh Johnson says: "Traces of pine resin have been found in amphorae from earliest times. It is usually assumed that it was used to preserve the wine, but resinated wine does not age well. The real reason is surely that Greek wine is much improved by the fresh, sappy, turpentine-like flavour which resin gives if added during the fermentation. The result is one of the most individual and appetizing drinks of the world."

Rhum French word for *Rum*.

Riesling The best German grape, "fine, fragrant, fruity" in the words of Hugh Johnson. Very extensively used in Germany, and the grape of the great and often expensive hocks.

Rioja (g) The wine-producing region which in Spain has the position of honour elsewhere conferred on Bordeaux and Burgundy. Rioja's best wines are its reds, a very pale version called clarete (like the French clairet), a dry version in a shouldered Bordeaux-style bottle, and a fuller version in a sloping-shouldered Burgundy-style bottle. Growers from Bordeaux came to Rioja in the 1870s, refugees from phylloxera until it caught up with them, but they implanted their techniques in Spain. Rioja wines are aged for a long time in wood, which lightens and smoothens the reds but can flatten the palate of the whites.

Rock and Rye (g) 30–35% Originally rock candy crystallized in rye whiskey. Today, rock candy syrup is used, with rye, grain, neutral spirits, and sometimes various fruits.

Ron Spanish word for *Rum*.

Rose, crème de (g) 30% Delicate liqueur produced from rose petals, with vanilla and sometimes citrus oils.

Rosé Pink, as always in wines and recently in a medium vermouth.

Rossi An Italian family which went into business with the *Martinis* to produce a famous *Vermouth*. Bitter Rossi (p) 25% is a delightful pink, vermouth-style patent apéritif from the same house.

Rosso Italian word for red, as applied to the Rosso (g) style of *Vermouth*. This is sweet, but less so than the *Bianco*. Rosso is the original Italian style of vermouth and remains the most popular in Italy.

Rum (g) 40–75.5% All spirits put notions into men's minds, and inspire mythology, but none more than rum, the very origins of which are lost in the smoke of cannon, the clatter of swords, and the clamour of mainbraces being spliced. It was the first national drink of the New World, the United States included, and the mythology says that the maritime frontiersmen sailed there on a sea of rum. No one is sure, amid the excitement, where the first rum was produced, or how it got its name. There is evidence to suggest that the name derives from a word in the dialect of maritime Devon, but it may just as well come from French, Spanish or even the Latin saccharum, meaning sugar. It was an Italian, none other than Christopher Columbus, who introduced sugar cane to the Caribbean, and almost every European nation involved itself in the West Indies. The Dutch even took rum to the East Indies (it became the first national spirit of Australia, too), and a Javanese version returned as a popular import to Sweden. The Scandinavians were also involved in the Caribbean, and a formerly Danish town now plays an important part in the German rum trade, where drinkers have a choice of the real thing or a rum-flavoured *Verschnitt*. Each colonizing nation had its own different procedures for the production of rum, in addition to which each territory's soil and climate has its own influence. Until the 1920s, the French regarded the three principal procedures as producing quite different drinks, and gave each a separate name. Today, it is all rum (or ron, or rhum, according to ethnicity). Nor can the name of an island or Latin American country be used to indicate a style of rum unless the product was actually made there. Although each rum country has its own traditional type, many today also mimic the styles of their competitors. Rum can be produced from two different raw materials: it can be distilled directly from the fermented juice of crushed sugar cane; or the sugar itself can first be extracted, and the rum made from the molasses which remain. A further variation entails the addition of *dunder*, which is residue from a previous distillation, to make a more pungent rum. Whichever raw materials are used, the duration of fermentation will also influence the final taste of the product. Then there is the means of distillation, since both pot and continuous stills are used. Traditionally, the French-speaking countries use the pot still to distil cane juice, on some occasions with dunder, into a high-quality rum of medium body. Among the English-speaking countries, Jamaica traditionally produces full-bodied rums from molasses and dunder in pot stills; Guyana produces its own distinctive style known as Demerara, which is dark but medium bodied, thanks to rapid fermentation, using molasses in continuous stills; Barbados uses both types of still to make its distinctively soft and smoky rum; and Trinidad produces medium-light rums in continuous stills. The Spanish-speaking countries produce light-bodied rums from molasses in continuous stills. Light-bodied rums do not require extensive ageing, those with a medium or full body may be matured in charred oak casks for anything from two to 15 years.

- **Rye (g)** 40–50% The first whiskey of the United States, probably dating back to the 1600s, though no one can be sure. Settlers from Scotland and Ireland had difficulty in growing good malting barley in their new homeland, but they had less trouble with rye. The Irish, at least, were already accustomed to using that in the production of whiskey. Those first distillers produced for themselves and their friends, and not on a commercial scale, and whiskey was not the significant spirit in the United States at that time; rum was. Rye was the tipple of the Pennsylvania and Maryland settlers, and it is still associated with those states. Sometimes, though, it seems that rye has never quite recovered from being upstaged by Kentucky *Bourbon*, which came later. That the first whiskey in the history of the United States should be relegated to being very much the second in public taste is a shame. Perhaps because it was the whiskey of the first settlers, rye has always lacked the glamour of bourbon. Perhaps because it has such character, a powerful palate and a full body, it has been mistakenly thought to be unsophisticated. Nor have American distillers and their marketing men helped by using such a confusion of semi-technical terms with which to describe the styles of their whiskeys. It is easy for the drinker to forget what is really what, and to neglect the fact that the United States offers him the choice of two distinct and distinctive indigenous whiskeys. Rye whiskey must be made with at least 51 per cent of the grain from which it takes its name, the rest being corn and barley, and is distilled in a continuous still. Like bourbon, it must be aged in new charred oak barrels for not less than a year, though in practice it is likely to be matured for much longer.

St Raphaël (p) 17% The sweetest of the major French patent apéritifs, in which some drinkers claim to detect a delectable hint of peaches.

Saké (g) 14–18% Not a spirit, though it is drunk short and tastes quite strong; not really a wine, though it is commonly described as rice wine; technically a beer, though that is what it least resembles. This ancient drink from Japan is not distilled; nor is it made from grapes; it is fermented, from rice. Saké is normally served quite warm, because heat releases its considerable bouquet. Grossman's Guide recommends the following procedure: "Place the opened bottle in a pot of boiling water. Remove it when the saké is about 100 to 105 degrees Fahrenheit. Decant the warm saké into small ceramic bottles called tokkuri. Pour into tiny porcelain bowls called sakazuki. The saké should be sipped. Often these sakazuki have a little tube on the outside, so that as you sip you draw in air and produce a whistling sound."

Sambuca (g) Approx 40% The flambé is the fun of sambuca. First float three or four coffee beans on top of a glass full of sambuca, then apply a flame to the liqueur. Let the flame dance for a few minutes until the coffee beans have sizzled and roasted, releasing an extra aroma into the sambuca, then blow it out as if it were candles on a cake. If you want to be really showy, lower the lights in the room before your performance, and explain to your guest(s) that the Italians say sambuca with coffee beans is "con mosche"— "with flies". For the lazy or modest, there is a variation of sambuca that comes already infused with coffee. Instead of being colourless, it is a dark brown, and labelled *negra*. Since the sharpness of the coffee offsets the stickiness of the sambuca, it is, as usual, deliciously indulgent to be lazy. There are many coffee liqueurs prepared to do double duty after dinner, but none quite as interesting as sambuca negra. Although it is a cousin of the French and Spanish sweet anis liqueurs, sambuca is made by an extraction method that provides a drier palate, and its distinctive ingredient is that of the elderbush. In its own country, sambuca is currently rather out of style. It is to be hoped that this foolish neglect stems merely from a temporary case of a prophet being without honour.

Sauternes (g) Just as chablis is the most famous white wine of Burgundy, so is sauternes of Bordeaux, but there is a catch. Ordinary sauternes is just another white wine, a pleasant drink for either before or after a meal, so long as it is served very cold. Only the famous châteaux, among which the most glittering, of course, is Yquem, can afford to make sauternes by the traditional method. To do this, it is necessary to pick over the vineyard as often as eight or nine times, to seek out those grapes blessed at various times through months of September to December with the so-called Noble Rot. Only these wizened grapes have the rich, sweet, scenty intensity which makes a true sauternes. Even then, it is only in the best of years that this will be possible.

Schnapps (g) To the rest of the world, schnapps vaguely means a "white" hard liquor drunk in northern Europe, perhaps a grainy tasting shot which is taken very cold in a short glass. The Dutch firm of Bols even make such a drink under the name of Aromatic Schnapps (p) in some markets, though the term is more commonly associated with Germany. There, usually spelled with only one "p", schnaps is an omnibus term for any hard liquor. If asked for a schnaps, a German bartender would either reel off a list of choices, or serve what he calls a *Korn* (g). This, too, is a vague term, but it usually refers to a clear grain spirit of excellent quality that has been distilled in a pot still in a manner intended to retain some of the flavour of the raw material, and that may have been matured by ageing. If the bartender offers a *Steinhäger* or *Wacholder* (g), he is referring to a spirit of this type that has been redistilled with crushed juniper berries, a splendid German version of gin. The korn spirit and its juniper brother, both being clear, are jointly bracketed as "klarer", and this is another term used by bartenders in Germany, and by drinkers when ordering. While klarer are most often the products of northern Germany, the original wacholder gin coming from the town of Steinhägen in the province of Westphalia, a request for schnapps elsewhere in the country might even elicit offers of a brandy from the Rhine or kirschwasser from the Black Forest.

Scotch (g) A whisky from Scotland and nowhere else. Scotch whisky cannot be made in England; no whisky is made anywhere in England. Scotch whisky cannot be made in the Americas or the Far East, though it can be imported for blending or bottling there. Most scotch whiskies are blended, often from the products of 50 or more distilleries. At least 60 per cent of a blend will usually comprise *Grain* whiskies, for cheapness and lightness, and the remainder a variety of malts from different parts of the country to achieve the particular balance between peatiness and smoothness, sweetness and dryness, which is sought by the brand in question. Cheap supermarket brands are always high on grain, and sometimes low on alcohol (though most blended scotches are sold at 40%). In the production of the light type of scotch favoured in the United States, the use of a high proportion of grain is one route, but the careful selection of reticent malts is another. The Scots themselves tend to go for slightly peaty blends, among which The Famous Grouse is a quite outstanding example. Bell's is the biggest-selling whisky in its home country, and the marginally maltier Teacher's in England. De luxe blends such as the excellent Chivas Regal and the lesser-known Old Parr have a higher content of malts. It is the pot-still malts that give Scotch its flavour. Some whiskies are made by the blending of several different malts, with no grain. These are known as *Vatted Malts*. An unblended *Malt Whisky* is described as being *Straight* or, more commonly, *Single*.

Seagram (p) The name of a whisky firm in Ontario, Canada, bought by the late Samuel Bronfman in 1926. By the early 1950s, Bronfman had made Seagram's into the world's biggest distilling group, and moved into a much-acclaimed new headquarters building, designed by Mies van der Rohe, in New York. Seagram's brands include Chivas Regal and, since 1977, The *Glenlivet*.

Sec, seco, secco (g) The words meaning dry in French, Spanish and Italian respectively.

Sekt (g) Nothing to do with dryness. Sekt is a generic term for German sparkling wines, many of which are fruitily sweet. Dry sekt is labelled Trocken.

• **Sherry (g)** 15–18% One of the world's fine wines and great apéritifs in its inimitable *Fino* form, and a richly versatile drink as an *Amontillado* or *Oloroso* (see separate entries). It is only a true sherry if it made in the Jerez region, though other countries hyphenate the style. Jerez de la Frontera is in the province of Cadiz, in Andalusia, southern Spain. In the course of its history, it has variously been known as Jerez, Xeres, Saris, Sherisch, Sherris and, especially by the English, Sherry. The wine that bears its name is fortified with brandy and is distinguished by two unusual processes in its production. One is a fermentation brought about by the action of an unusual yeast, *flor*, which forms a film on the surface of the wine. Flor can live in higher amounts of alcohol than other yeasts, and it imparts a special flavour to the wine. The other distinctive aspect of sherry production is the system of ageing and blending. In the bodega, the wine is kept in ranks of wooden butts, anything from 20 to 100, and is transferred from one to another by jug until it has passed through the whole system, which is known as a *solera*. At one end of the system, young wine is added; at the other end, mature wine is drawn. Since all the wine in the system is of the same category, it is further blended during the further processes which take place before shipping. The production of sherry is complex, painstaking and infinitely subtle; when the Moors nurtured viniculture in southern Spain a thousand years ago, they did a service to the world.

Shrub (g) A home-made drink produced by the maceration of fruits in alcohol (see Mixed Drinks section, page 135) and a patent cordial of low alcoholic content from the west of England.

Single (g) Scottish colloquial term for a *Straight malt whisky*.

Slivovitz, various spellings (g) 40–50% Distinctive style of good-quality plum brandy made in various countries of Central Europe and the Balkans, and regarded as the national spirit of Yugoslavia. Slivovitz is made from the large, sweet Pozega plum of Bosnia, and the trees are not cropped for this purpose until they are a mature 20 years old. Part of the kernel is used, producing a characteristically dry almond bitterness and oiliness which some drinkers find unpleasant, but which on the tongues of Central European connoisseurs is likely to prompt cries of Na Zdorov'e or Mazeltov! A further characteristic of Slivovitz, which distinguishes it from the equally admirable plum brandies of the *Eau-de-vie* country, is the method of ageing. Slivovitz is aged in wood, hence its yellowish colour with a tinge of brown.

Sloe gin (g) 25%+ A very English and rather rural drink for the flasks of fox-hunting folk. A *Gin* because that is what the sloe berries, and sometimes other fruit flavourings, are macerated in. Sloe gin is matured in wood.

Sour mash (g) Although this process is proclaimed strongly on the label of *Jack Daniel's* excellent product, a sour mash is used by many American distillers in the production of *Bourbon*. The residue from a previous fermentation is added to the new mash to assist continuity of character and reinforce the flavour and bouquet.

Southern Comfort (p) 50% One of the few indigenous American liqueurs, and surely the oldest. Said to have been derived from a cocktail of peaches and *Bourbon*, which was in turn invented either in New Orleans or in St Louis, Missouri, where Southern Comfort is produced. It took Southern Comfort a while to cross the Mason-Dixon line, but it is now a modish drink all over the world. In addition to the peaches, it has a hint of oranges and herbs, and it is relatively dry and strong for a liqueur. More of a flavoured whiskey, suitable for sunny afternoons in mixed drinks and early evenings on the rocks, though some drinkers like it after dinner.

Spanish brandies (g) 40% In Europe, the consensus would probably say that Spanish brandy, in its own rather ebullient way, is second only to French, though it lacks the pedigree of armagnac or the finesse of cognac. It is sweeter than either, deceptively and dangerously heavy, but at its best very smooth. Though they are in most cases distilled from the wines of La Mancha, around Valdepeñas, south of Madrid, Spanish brandies are often matured and marketed by the sherry shippers of Jerez.

Spumante (g) Italian term for sparkling wine. See *Asti*.

Steam Beer (g) Approx 5% The only indigenous beer of the United States. Traditionally said to release

83

a great deal of steam-like pressure when the casks are tapped. Produced by a hybrid process devised to make a *Lager*-type beer in breweries that did not have the necessary cooling. The result resembles an *Ale*, but has a character and individuality that are all its own. The tradition is splendidly carried on by the Anchor Steam Brewery (p) in San Francisco.

Steinhäger (g) 30–35% Excellent German *Gin* made by a most unusual method. Crushed juniper berries are made into a mash and fermented, then distilled. The resultant spirit is then redistilled with neutral alcohol in a pot still. No botanical flavourings are used other than a small quantity of dried juniper berries, which is added in a manner rather reminiscent of the dry-hopping of beer. Despite the use of the berries as both a fermentable material and a flavouring, their influence in the palate of the end product is surprisingly subtle. The product is commonly ordered as steinhäger, after the town in West-phalia where it traditionally is made, though its generic name is wacholder.

Stout (g) 3–7.5% A top-fermented beer made with highly roasted, and sometimes unmalted, barley. Although stouts are brewed on a small scale else-where in the world, they are most commonly found in the British Isles, where a clear distinc-tion is made between the sweet type of low alcoholic content such as England's Mackeson (p) and the stronger dry type such as Ireland's Guinness (p).

Stonsdorfer (p) 32% A good-quality digestif bitters from Germany.

Straight whisky, whiskey With reference to scotch, a whisky that has not been blended in any way. In the United States, a distiller who puts together more than one mature *Bourbon* or *Rye* may describe the result as a blended straight whiskey. This contradiction in terms distinguishes his pro-duct from a blend of bourbon or rye with an inferior whiskey or neutral spirit.

•**Strega (p)** 40% When two people drink strega, they are forever united, according to one of those legends that so conveniently cobweb the liqueur houses of Italy. It is a magic drink, from a recipe created by beautiful maidens who for reasons unexplained disguised themselves as witches. This typically Italian liqueur, sweet and spicy, made from more than 70 herbs, is none the worse for its mythology. It is a rich after-dinner drink, useful in cocktails, and the flavouring in a famous Italian ice-cream.

Suze (p) 17%+ Extremely idiosyncratic French bitter apéritif, yellow, with a powerful flavour of gentian root. Drunk with lots of ice, soda and sometimes lemon juice, or straight by the brave.

Swedish Punsch (g) 30%+ One of the odder drinks in the Western World, though its origins are Eastern. In a throwback to the days when the northern Europeans traded extensively with the East Indies, the Swedes still drink as a local speciality a ready-made punch based on the rum-type arrak of Java. What the Swedes term simply punsch is a ready-bottled mélange of arrak, neutral spirit, and various wines, aged for some months. The Swedes drink this hot with their winter pea soup, or as liqueur.

Tarragona Town and region in Catalonia where several types of fortified wine are produced.

Tennessee whiskey (g) 45% A *Straight whiskey* produced in Tennessee from at least 51 per cent of a single grain. In practice, the famous Tennessee whiskeys are in the *bourbon* style, using the sour mash process, with charcoal filtration.

Tequila (g) 40%+ The spirit of the 1970s, and perhaps of the 1980s, since its potential as both a hard liquor of ritualistic machismo and a cocktail base seems far from exhausted. The sun will continue to rise, Margarita will continue to bestow her salty kisses, but there is surely much more to come. Tequila itself took a long time in coming. The first recorded shipment across the border was in 1873. The tax records of the town of Tequila say that three barrels of "mezcal wine" were sent from Mexico to New Mexico. Tequila was also taken home by the American troops who fought in the 1916 clash, though their adversary Pancho Villa was himself a fanatical teetotaller. The spirit certainly crossed the border during the Prohibition period, too, and began to gain a tiny cult following in the United States during the post-war period, especially the 1950s. The Californians might well argue on historical grounds that tequila has always been their national spirit, and it was students in Los Angeles who made the drink fashionable in the late 1960s. Its broader popularity came with a concerted commercial effort, but the brands which paved the way for that success were sadly bland by Mexican standards. This says more about the neutrality of American taste than it does about the lack of sophistication in the Mexican distilling industry, though the urbane cocktail-mixer David Embury argues that the purpose of the salt-and-lime routine is to counteract the ripe odour of basic tequila. Surely the ritual has more to do with the refreshment of body and soul on a hot, dry day, a continuous process which renders meaningless and interminable arguments as to which is the proper order in which to proceed. Suck a lime, knock back a Tequila, and lick the pinch of salt which you have placed on the back of your hand. Now try it while chewing tobacco. The spirit of Mexico is made from the sap of the mezcal, variously known as the century or argarth plant, or described as a type of aloe, of the genus agave or maguey, and not truly a cactus. The particular variety that grows around the town of Tequila, in Jalisco state, and in four neighbouring states, produces the best mezcal spirit. Tequila is to mezcal as cognac is to brandy. The town itself is 40 miles west of Guadalajara, amid the Sierra Madre Occidental mountains. Traditionally, Tequila is double-distilled, and a pot still is used. The best is aged either in wax-lined tanks or oak casks, though rarely for more than four years.

Tia Maria (p) 30%+ An old-established coffee liqueur based on rum, and flavoured with Jamaican spices. Made in Jamaica with Blue Mountain coffee, and drier than *Kahlúa*.

Tokay Various spellings, and various meanings, the original of which is a famous strong, sweet white wine made in a small area around the village of Tokaj, in Hungary. Tokay is made from Furmint grapes, and the Noble Rot plays a part as it does in Sauternes. The finest tokay has been known to mature for 250 years. The word tokay is also used to describe an unrelated grape originating from Algeria, and a blended dessert wine made in California with a sherry flavour.

Triple Sec (g) 30–40% Not as dry as it sounds, but one of the most refined forms of *Curaçao*.

Van der Hum (g) 30% South African liqueur made from local naartje tangerines, with herbs.

Vandermint (p) 30% Mint chocolate liqueur from The Netherlands, marketed in Delft-style bottles.

Vanilla The beans are occasionally used in mixed drinks. Crème de vanille is smooth and rich.

Vatted malt whisky (g) 40–57% Scottish term for *Whisky* blended only from *Single malts*, with no grain. Examples include Strathconon, Berry's All Malt and Kiltarity.

Vermouth (g) 16–18% From the German *wermut*, meaning wormwood, though none of the misconceived odium aimed at *Absinthe* has affected this innocent Franco-Italian genre of apéritif. Within a glass of vermouth is the whole history of alcoholic confection. First and foremost, it is the ultimate in treated wine, and that is a product which dates back to the ancients; there still survives equipment which was used by the Romans to aromatize their wines, both as a means of improving their flavour and of preservation. Then again, vermouth is the ultimate in complicated herbal recipes. The countless herbs used in vermouths include all of the great favourites that occur in bitters (often made by the same companies) and in liqueurs: camomile in dry vermouth, gentian in red, vanilla in sweet, along with Chinese rhubarb, iris root, quinine, citrus peels and at least 150 others. Somehow the craft survived through the Dark Ages and reappeared in the hands of monks, alchemists and doctors. Herbal remedies have never ceased to be widely used in France and more specially Italy, and the shop that supplies the roots, bark, seeds, berries and flowers sells them equally to the home physic and the domestic liqueurist. Though many of the typical ingredients are obtainable only from the Far East and Latin America, many others grow in the Alps. It was there, on both sides of the mountain ranges, and therefore on both sides of the Franco-Italian frontier, that the production of liqueurs and vermouths, especially the latter, became an industry: in France, at Chambéry, famous for dry and delicate vermouths, at Lyon, whence *Noilly* moved to Marseilles, still not far from the Alps, and at Grenoble; in Italy, at Turin, the biggest vermouth-producing city of all, home of both *Martini* and *Cinzano*, and at Milan, where the term vermouth was invented by Carpano. Each vermouth is still made in a slightly different way, though all are macerated, for periods of between six months and a year or more. Some are partially the product of distillation, notably the dry type, which is the strongest. All types of vermouth are extensively used in cocktails, and as aperitifs, usually with plenty of ice, and sometimes with soda.

Vichy Célestins (p) Famous salty mineral water from the French spa town of Vichy, north of Clermont Ferrand. If water can be dry, Vichy is.

Vieille Curé (p) 43% Well known for its "stained glass" packaging, though that might distract attention from the qualities of this typically excellent French liqueur, produced at the Abbey of Cenon, Bordeaux. Taking advantage of its perfect location between the Cognac and Armagnac areas, La Vieille Curé uses both in which to macerate its 50 herbal ingredients. The green and yellow varieties have slightly different palates but the same alcohol content.

Violette, crème de (g) 25–40% Made from the petals of violets, sometimes with additional flavour from *Curaçao* oranges.

• **Vodka (g)** 35–80% A misunderstood and rather misrepresented term. In Slavic countries, vodka is a generic term for any spirit drink, whether it is distilled from grape, grain, potato or whatever. The word is simply an ironic diminutive for water. In Poland and Russia these spirits are available in a wide variety of spiced and fruit versions, and even in the unflavoured vodkas a degree of grain palate is sometimes deliberately retained, perhaps enhanced by ageing. The most celebrated example of a delicately flavoured vodka is Zubrowka, with a blade of grass in every bottle. The grass is of the type favoured by the wild European bison, which grazes on the borders of Poland and Russia. Of the unflavoured vodkas, Tony Lord says in *The World Guide to Spirits*: "The bouquet of a clear eastern vodka is spirity, with a light oiliness. The flavour is strong and almost 'green'." It was none the less the early skill of the Slavs in producing very thoroughly distilled unflavoured vodkas that inspired the idea of a neutral spirit as a basis for mixed drinks. The original purpose of this rectification was to produce a strong spirit that would not readily freeze in extreme weather. Alcohol freezes at a lower point than water. It was this rationale which produced the world's strongest commercially marketed liquor, Polish pure spirit (p) 80%. At a less ferocious level, the popularity of Smirnoff as a flag-carrier for neutral vodkas has compounded the dispute between the Poles and Russians over the origins of that type of drink. If vodka is taken to mean a highly rectified and distilled neutral spirit with little or no flavour, as used in mixed drinks, where was it invented? Perhaps Smirnoff can provide the answer. Smirnoff originates from the city of Lvov, which has through most of its history been regarded as being Polish, but which is now in the Soviet Union. Though they all look and taste much the same, "Western" vodkas are distilled from a wide variety of raw materials, ranging from beet in Turkey, and often molasses in Britain, to grain in the United States. Products which yield sugar distil very well, yet grain somehow has more respectability with the drinker; it really doesn't matter, and neutral vodka will always be distilled from what is available.

Weisse Bier (g) 2.5–3% "White" beer for which Berlin is famous, and which was once made in Philadelphia. Three parts of barley to one of wheat produce a very unusual light and sparkling beer for summer. Served in a large bowl-shaped glass with, astonishingly, a dash of raspberry juice or essence of woodruff, producing lurid colours, and offered with a straw.

Weizen Bier (g) 5% "Wheat" beer from the south of Germany, notably Stuttgart. From a third to two-thirds of the mash is made with wheat, and the palate is slightly fruity. Served in a tall vase-shaped glass, with a slice of lemon.

Whisky, whiskey 40–60% Always spelled without the "e" in Scotland, and with it in the United States. Canada usually goes the Scottish way, and Ireland generally uses the "e". Each of the whisky-producing countries has its own style, for which it sets standards, but where does whisky begin and end? Consensus would seem to say that whisky is a spirit drink distilled from grain, including a proportion of barley malt, which retains a pronounced flavour from its raw materials. This flavour may be heightened by the method of malting used (as in peaty scotches) or by the type of cask used for ageing. Whisky is an abbreviation and familiarization of uisge, and that of uisge beatha or usquebaugh, all being Gaelic for water of life. See *Scotch, Irish, Bourbon, Rye,* etc.

White rum (g)40% Colourless rum of the light-bodied type produced in continuous stills. See *Rum.*

Wild Turkey (p) Brand-name used on a high-quality straight *Bourbon whiskey* (50.5%) and a rather sweet bourbon liqueur (40%), both made by Austin, Nichols.

Yvette, crème (p) Violet-petal liqueur made in honour of the French actress Yvette Gilbert at the turn of the century. The best-known liqueur of this type, by Jacquin, of Philadelphia.

Cocktails and other mixed drinks

"A nicer discrimination ... refined taste ... the more genial customs which we have been led to adopt through our constant intercourse with France and other countries ... led to a beneficial change in our bibulous doings," according to a charming work on mixed drinks produced in London around 1870.

That book clearly perceived as the original mixed drinks the claret cups of Bordeaux, the ratafias of Savoy, perhaps the vermouths of Piedmont, the latter doing much to modify the rough gins of the day. It also recognized, though, that the idea had already spread west in "those notions, many of which—owing to their racy character—are properly styled 'sensations' by our Yankee cousins".

A confusion of terms was employed to describe the various types of mixed drink: cobbler, cooler, crusta, cup, daisy, fix, flip, julep, negus, nog, sangaree, sling, smash, rickey, posset, punch. Most of these terms are still in use, and the distinctions between them remain a matter of disagreement.

Another type of mixed drink described in that book of 1870 was "the cocktail—not so ancient an institution as juleps, etcetera, but with its next of kin 'crusta', promises to maintain its ground". The typical recipe quoted specified a tablespoon of bitters, half a gill of ginger syrup, half a gill of curaçao, and a quarter-pint of gin, stirred and served over ice in a tumbler, the rim of which had been moistened with lemon juice.

There are now about 10,000 mixed drinks recognized by the New York Bartenders' Guild, and there have been many more over the years, though the overwhelming majority are minor variations on a few great themes. Even the idea of a classic or standard mixed drink—of which any bartender can be expected to know—varies with fashion. In the list which follows, standard cocktails are marked★

There are almost as many explanations for the term cocktail, all rather unlikely, and some decidedly tongue-in-cheek.

Unable to leave Dr Johnson out of it, the British enthusiast John Doxat attributes to him a contrived story about horses of mixed blood having cocked tails. In the American war of independence, tavern-keeper Betsy Flanagan, widow of a Revolutionary soldier, is supposed to have stolen the tail feathers from a Tory neighbour's cock and used them to decorate drinks. Several stories link mixed drinks with cock-fighting lore. The feathers were allegedly used to stir mixed drinks served to Mississippi gamblers, or was it British sailors in the Gulf of Mexico? Then there was the story of the drink mixed by a beautiful Mexican girl called Coctel; surely that fits the spirit of the tequila age?

It was the jazz age that passed the cocktail into folk history, as a disguise for bootleg liquor, and Harry Craddock, the proponent of the Coctel story, who brought the mixing of drinks back across the Atlantic. His scholarly work at the Savoy Hotel in London elevated the serving of cocktails to the status of high art.

Although the word cocktail is often used loosely to describe all types of mixed drink, it does have a more specific meaning. Among the many names applied to various types of alcoholic confection, the term cocktail is applied with precision to a short apéritif (and therefore a dry drink) based on a predominant hard spirit.

In such drinks, the base spirit should be tasted, and usually accounts for at least half the content. Some of the recipes which follow may be judged to be generous with hard liquor; they can always be scaled down as the evening goes on. In any event, a trial run is urged before anything new is tried on guests. Between 12 and 16 mixed drinks should be obtainable from what the British call simply a bottle and the Americans a "fifth".

Brand-names of ingredients are given in the following list only where the originator of the recipe expressed a preference. Almost all liqueurs will considerably sweeten a drink, but many recipes call for further sugar in various forms. Although this is a matter of the originator's preference, sugar syrup (known in Britain by the brand-name Gomme Syrup) dissolves the easiest. This can be made by simmering a pound of sugar in a pint of water. Once it has cooled down, the solution can be bottled and kept in the cocktail cabinet or bar. The sweeter drinks are singled out with the symbol ♥

Truly short drinks are identified by the symbol ▼ , and anything longer is marked ▌ .

For the best chilling, put the ice in first. To avoid waste and keep tabs on what drinks you are mixing, put the base spirit in last. Craftily spray soda into the ice-bucket to keep the cubes separate, warm in advance anything that is to be flambéed, and have a good time.

Aberdeen Angus Restores the energy after a strenu-
ous few hours on the grouse moors. Although
scotch whisky has too delicate a palate to work
well in many mixed drinks, this one was made for
it. Single malt seems a sinful extravagance in a
mixed drink anyway, and a Highland might be
more geographically appropriate, but a really
peaty Islay makes for a truly distinctive drink.

*2 oz scotch whisky, 1 oz Drambuie, 1 tablespoon
honey, 2 tablespoons lime juice.*

Stir the scotch, honey and lime juice in a drinking
mug until they are blended. Warm the Drambuie
in a ladle over a low flame. Ignite it, and pour the
burning liqueur into the mug. Stir vigorously, and
drink immediately from the mug.

Absinthe Suissesse For absinthe, pour Pernod.
Both, of course, originated in Switzerland. Non-
Gallic drinkers sometimes find Pernod a little
heavy, and it is lightened delightfully in this pre-
or post-prandial cocktail, which was probably
invented not in Europe but in Louisiana.

*1½ oz Pernod or other anis, 2 or 3 drops anisette,
2 or 3 drops orange-flower water, a modest
teaspoon white crème de menthe or peppermint
schnapps, 1 egg white.*

Shake with ice, and strain into a cocktail glass.

Acapulco A potent and robust restorative after the
pleasures of a hot day. This tequila version seems
most appropriate, although another recipe employs triple sec and uses the white of an egg.

*1½ oz tequila, 1½ oz Jamaica rum, 3 oz pineapple
juice, 1 oz (or slightly less) grapefruit or lime
juice, cubes of fresh pineapple (optional).*

Shake with ice cubes, and serve on the rocks in a
Collins glass, garnished with the pineapple.

★ ***Admiral*** Jazz-lovers may respond best to Benny
Goodman's version of this old standard, although
he is uncharacteristically heavy-handed when it
comes to vermouth.

*1 oz bourbon, 2 oz dry vermouth, juice of ½ lemon,
a twist of lemon peel.*

Shake well with ice. Serve on the rocks in an Old
Fashioned glass, decorated with the twist.

Adonis A classic cocktail which is a splendid apéritif.
Some barmen prefer to use orange bitters.

*2 oz dry sherry, 1 oz sweet Italian vermouth,
2 dashes Angostura bitters.*

Stir well with ice, and strain into a cocktail glass.

★ ***Affinity*** The traditional recipe, as set out in *The
Savoy Cocktail Book*, uses scotch whisky with
equal parts of dry and sweet vermouth, and

dashes of Angostura bitters. Trader Vic's version, given here, is more fun.

½ oz dry French vermouth, ½ oz sweet Italian vermouth, ¼ oz crème de violette.

Shake with ice, and strain into a cocktail glass.

Akvavit Clam One of those apéritifs which feeds the drinker while at the same time rousing his appetite to further challenges.

3 oz Danish akvavit, 1½ oz clam juice, 1½ oz tomato juice, 1 teaspoon lemon juice, ½ teaspoon Worcestershire sauce, a sprinkling of salt, black pepper and cayenne pepper.

Stir vigorously in a mixing glass, chill thoroughly. Serve with ice in an Old Fashioned glass.

Alaska An excuse to get out the Chartreuse for a good old glamorous cocktail before dinner or the theatre. Opinions vary over the quantities, but too much Chartreuse makes for a sweet drink.

2 oz (or even more) London Dry gin, ½ oz (or even less) green Chartreuse, ½ oz dry sherry (optional), a twist of lemon peel.

Stir thoroughly with ice cubes, and strain into a cocktail glass. Decorate with the lemon peel.

Alcudia Galliano has featured in many cocktails since it was popularized by being used in the Harvey Wallbanger. This example is teasingly sweet and dry.

2 oz dry gin, 1 oz Galliano, 1 oz crème de banane, 1 oz grapefruit juice, a twist of grapefruit peel.

Shake with ice cubes, and strain into a cocktail glass. Decorate with the grapefruit peel.

Ale flip Can be drunk chilled, but is better as a hot drink. Best with a bitter but full-bodied British brew, although good results have been obtained with American ales such as Rainier, from Seattle, or even with Steam Beer. Serves four.

1 quart ale, 2 egg whites, 4 egg yolks, 4 tablespoons sugar, nutmeg.

Bring the ale gently to the boil in a saucepan. Beat the egg whites until they are frothy. Beat the yolks, and mix with the whites and the sugar. Pour the mixture very slowly into the beer, stirring vigorously. Pour the beer to and fro between two pans several times to create a frothy head. Serve in fireproof mugs, with a dusting of nutmeg.

Alexander See *Brandy Alexander*

Alfonso Cocktail For those blasé folk who genuinely feel that neat champagne is rather boring.

2 tablespoons Dubonnet, 1 dash Angostura or Peychaud's bitters, 1 lump sugar, champagne, a twist of lemon peel.

Put the sugar in a large, saucer-shaped champagne glass, and sprinkle with bitters. Add the Dubonnet and 1 ice cube, then fill with well-chilled champagne, and decorate with the twist.

★*Alfonso Special* The Grand Marnier makes this an
Y interesting sweet-and-dry experience

1½ oz Grand Marnier, ¾ oz dry gin, ¾ oz dry vermouth, 4 dashes sweet vermouth, 1 dash Angostura bitters.

Stir well with ice, and strain into a cocktail glass.

Algonquin A cocktail to inspire literary witticisms.
Y Wouldn't Dorothy Parker have agreed that liquor is quicker?

2 oz rye, 1 oz dry vermouth, 1 oz pineapple juice.

Shake with ice, and serve on the rocks in an Old Fashioned glass.

All-White Frappé Virginally pretty, and rather
Y sweet, especially if crème de menthe is preferred.
♥ *1 oz peppermint schnapps, 1 oz white crème de cacao, 1 oz anisette, 1 oz lemon juice.*

Shakes with ice cubes, and strain over crushed ice in a cocktail glass.

Amaretto Heartwarmer A new recipe, loosely based
Y on the Almond Cocktail.

2 oz Southern Comfort, 1 oz dry vermouth, 1 oz Amaretto, 2 blanched almonds, 1 crushed peach kernel, ½ teaspoon sugar.

Warm the Southern Comfort. Add the almonds, kernel and sugar, and stir. Allow to cool. Add the Amaretto, and stir. Strain over lots of ice in an Old Fashioned glass.

Ambassador Barely a cocktail, but a simple and
▌ effective refresher.

2 oz tequila, fresh orange juice to taste, 1 teaspoon sugar syrup, 1 slice orange.

Stir. Serve on the rocks in an Old Fashioned or Collins glass, garnished with the orange slice.

Amer Picon Cocktail Several delicious apéritifs are
Y served under this name. In one version the Amer Picon is simply laced with a teaspoon of grenadine and Perrier is added to taste. In another, the juice of 1 lime is added to this mixture. Trader Vic's recipe comes with a guarantee that it will arouse hunger.

¾ oz Amer Picon, ¾ oz sweet Italian vermouth.

Shake with ice cubes, and strain into a chilled cocktail glass.

★*American Beauty* All things nice are in this classic
Y cocktail. Perhaps that is why, imbibed in modera-
♥ tion, it settles both the stomach and the mind.

¾ oz brandy, ¾ oz dry vermouth, ¾ oz orange juice,

94

¼ oz white crème de menthe or peppermint schnapps, a dash of grenadine, 1 oz port.

Shake all the ingredients except the port with crushed ice. Strain into an Old Fashioned or cocktail glass. Tilt the glass, and slowly add the port so that it floats on top.

Americano An Italiano, really. One of those sunny apéritifs that is also very refreshing.

¾ oz Campari, ¾ oz Italian sweet vermouth, soda to taste, 1 slice orange.

Stir well in an Old Fashioned glass generously loaded with ice cubes. Garnish with the orange slice. May also be made in a very large *ballon* wine glass.

Aperitif Perrier Converts a hard day at the top into a healthy appetite. Long before America discovered Perrier it was a favourite in Europe, not only for its natural sparkle but also for its stomach-settling qualities. Purists may object to the addition of alcohol, but Perrier was made famous by an Englishman, A. W. St John Harmsworth, so it should go well with London Dry and French.

1½ oz London Dry gin, 1½ oz Noilly Prat, ½ oz Rose's lime juice (or 3 oz fresh lime or grapefruit juice), Perrier, a twist of cucumber peel.

Shake the liquor and fruit juice very thoroughly with ice cubes, and strain into a *ballon* wine glass, or Collins glass, over 2 or 3 ice cubes. Top up with Perrier. Decorate with the cucumber peel.

Apple Toddy For autumn evenings. Tastes better if the apple is marinated in the brandy for two or three days, but this is not essential.

1 cooking apple, 1 bottle apple brandy, 1½ oz grape or other fruit brandy according to taste, 4 lemon slices stuck with cloves, 1 stick cinnamon, 1 tablespoon sugar.

Bake the apple and remove the skin. In each of 4 fireproof glasses, place a quarter of the apple pulp, a sprinkling of sugar, a slice of lemon, and a piece of cinnamon. Pour on the brandy. Top up with boiling water, and stir.

Applejack Punch Many recipes. This one serves a couple of dozen experienced drinkers.

2 bottles applejack, 1 pint lemon juice, 1 pint orange juice, 6 oz grenadine, 2 large bottles ginger ale, apple slices, mint sprigs.

Stir all the ingredients except the ginger ale vigorously with lots of chunky ice in a punch bowl. Add ginger ale just before serving. Decorate with the apple slices and mint sprigs.

★**Applejack Rabbit** There are applejack cocktails made with curaçao or sweet vermouth, and there is the Rabbit, which is both decorative and tasty.

1½ oz apple brandy, ½ oz lemon juice, ½ oz lime or orange juice, according to taste, ½ teaspoon maple syrup.

Shake thoroughly with ice. Dip the rim of an Old Fashioned glass in maple syrup, and line it with sugar. Strain the Rabbit into the glass over lots of ice.

Atholl Brose Not so much the original oatmeal drink as an extremely Scottish dessert which has attained a certain chic in English dining circles.

1½ oz scotch whisky, 1½ oz clear honey, 1½ oz double cream.

Mix well in a warm glass or ramekin. Allow to cool, and chill.

Aztec Punch Tequila packs the punch, of course. Serves about twenty.

1 gallon tequila, 5 gallons grapefruit juice, 2 quarts dark tea, 3 cups lemon juice, 1 cup sugar syrup.

Stir together in a punch bowl, with large blocks of ice.

★**Bacardi Special** The best known among the several cocktails that insist on the Bacardi brand. A Daiquiri variation.

2 oz Bacardi rum, ¾ oz gin, the juice of 1 small lime, a dash of grenadine, ½ teaspoon sugar.

Shake all the ingredients except the rum with cracked ice until cold. Add the rum, shake again until cold. Strain into a cocktail glass.

Baltimore Egg Nog There are numerous recipes for this party stand-by.

1 oz cognac or other brandy, 1½ oz madeira, ½ oz Jamaica rum, 2 teaspoons sugar syrup, 1 egg, 4 oz fresh milk, 2 oz double cream, nutmeg.

Shake vigorously with ice cubes. Strain into a Collins glass. Top up with cold milk, and dust with grated nutmeg.

Banana Bird Lovers of the fruit itself may have more fun in the Daiquiri department, but the Banana Bird is an interesting, if unpretentious, cocktail.

1 oz bourbon, 2 teaspoons crème de banane, 2 teaspoons triple sec (Cointreau is a good example), 1 oz double cream.

Shake with ice, and strain into a cocktail glass.

Beer Sangaree A simpler drink than a flip. Sangarees are more commonly made with wine.

½ pint strong ale or porter, 1 to 2 teaspoons sugar syrup or sugar, nutmeg.

Lightly chill the beer. Place the sugar in a Collins glass, add a little water, stir, pour on the beer, and dust with grated nutmeg.

Bellini From Harry's Bar in Venice, a film-crowd
favourite in the "swinging sixties". For lazy afternoons and beautiful people. Serves four.
1 bottle champagne, 3 or 4 peaches, a sprinkling of sugar.
Purée the peaches, thoroughly chill the champagne, and stir together gently in a punch bowl until blended. Decant into elegant glasses.

Bermuda Rose There is also the Bouquet, but the
single Rose is the best-known Bermuda cocktail.
1½oz gin, 1 tablespoon lime juice, 2 or 3 drops each of apricot brandy and grenadine.
Shake with ice cubes, and strain over ice into an Old Fashioned glass.

Betsy Ross Revives the spirit and settles the stomach.
Some argue that the brandy should be Spanish, and in much greater quantity.
1½oz brandy, 1oz port, ½ teaspoon Cointreau, dash of Angostura bitters.
Shake with ice cubes, and strain into an Old Fashioned glass, with ice cubes.

Between the Sheets A classic, despite its rather vulgar
name.
1oz Cointreau, 1oz brandy, 1oz white rum, 1oz lime juice (optional), 1 twist lemon peel.
Shake with cracked ice, strain into a saucer-shaped champagne glass, and decorate with the lemon peel.

Big Apple You drink out of the apple in the most
colourful version of this summery "I love New York" potion.
1 eating apple, 3oz apple brandy, 2oz orange juice, 1oz lemon juice.
Cut a hole in the top of the apple and scoop out the core and enough of the pulp to make plenty of room for the drink. Place the apple shell in the ice-making compartment of the refrigerator for about 15 minutes. Meanwhile, mix the rest of the ingredients very thoroughly indeed with the apple pulp in a blender. Strain into the apple shell, and serve with a straw—or two.

The Bishop A wine drink made with baked orange,
and usually served hot. Variations include The Cardinal (claret) and The Pope (champagne). This one is called The English Bishop. Serves six.
1 large orange, 12 cloves, 1 quart inexpensive port, 1 tablespoon honey, 1 teaspoon allspice (optional), a few dashes of cognac.

Stick the cloves into the orange, and bake it in a slow oven for about 30 minutes. Cut the baked orange into quarters, and put in a pan with all the remaining ingredients. Simmer over a very low flame for 20 minutes. Do not boil. Serve in heated cups.

★**Black Russian** A stylish after-dinner cocktail which
Y may be made less sweet by the addition of a drop or two of lemon juice, in which case it becomes a Black Magic. For those unsociable enough to smoke after dinner, a Sobranie cigarette is appropriate.
1½ oz vodka, ¾ oz Kahlúa or Tia Maria.
Shake with ice, and strain into a cocktail glass.

Blackthorn, English Being the fruit of the black-
Y thorn, surely it is only right that the sloe should flavour this cocktail? Sloe gin may be half-forgotten, but it does have a wistful English charm.
1 oz sloe gin, 1 oz (or less) Italian sweet vermouth, ½ oz Plymouth gin (optional), 2 dashes orange bitters.
Stir with ice, and strain into a cocktail glass.

Blackthorn, Irish To be sure, isn't a blackthorn a
Y shillelagh, and therefore a Hibernian invention?
1½ oz Irish whiskey, 1½ oz dry vermouth, 3 dashes Pernod, 3 dashes Angostura bitters.
Stir with ice cubes, and serve on the rocks in an Old Fashioned glass.

Black Velvet The most delicious Gaelic-Gallic con-
▌ spiracy since Wolfe Tone's rather more political essay. Wonderful for an outdoor party on a summer's afternoon.
Equal parts of champagne or good-quality sparkling wine (must be very dry) and bitter stout (Guinness, Murphy or Beamish).
Chill all the ingredients, then pour them simultaneously into a large pitcher, and decant into the tallest glasses you can find.

Blended Comfort One of many excellent mixed
▌ drinks made with Southern Comfort.
1 oz Southern Comfort, 2 oz bourbon, ½ oz dry vermouth, 1 oz orange juice, 2 tablespoons lemon juice, 4 oz crushed ice, ¼ peach plus 1 peach slice, 1 orange slice.
Skin the peach quarter. Mix the ingredients in a blender at low speed for 10 to 15 seconds. Strain over crushed ice in a Collins glass. Decorate with the peach slice and orange slice.

★**Bloody Mary** Surely the drink that did most to popu-
98 ▌ larize the Western version of vodka, notwith-

standing the inevitable later variations using other spirits. Everyone has an opinion on the Bloody Mary. In *The Fine Art of Mixing Drinks*, David Embury describes it as "a classic example of combining in one potion both the poison and the antidote". Gourmet and restaurateur Robert Carrier adds sherry and celery salt. Blender-freaks have even been known to use celery leaves and the white of an egg. It depends whether you want a drink or a meal.

1½ oz vodka, 1 small tin tomato juice (about 3 oz), ½ oz lemon juice, 1 bar spoon Worcestershire sauce, 2 drops Tabasco (optional), salt and pepper, 1 lemon slice (optional).

Shake with 3 ice cubes and strain into an Old Fashioned glass, or a *ballon* wine glass, with salt and pepper to taste. If you like, decorate with a slice of lemon.

Blue Blazer A spectacular and extremely difficult, not to mention dangerous, drink to serve.

1 teaspoon or more sugar (or 1 tablespoon honey), 4 oz warmed scotch, a twist of lemon peel or nutmeg.

Warm two ½ pint metal tankards or mugs. In one, dissolve the sugar or honey in about 3 oz boiling water. Pour the scotch into the other and set it alight. While it is blazing, pour the scotch back and forth from one mug to the other, to create a continuous stream of fire. When the flame dies down, pour the liquid into a heated wine glass. Decorate with lemon, or dust with nutmeg.

Blue Hawaiian A colourful concoction which causes geographical confusion by coming from the Zanzibar Club, London. An after-office drink for smart young things.

½ oz blue curaçao, 2 oz Bacardi, 1 oz pineapple juice, 1 teaspoon coconut cream. Shake with ice cubes, and strain into a cocktail glass.

Bolo See *English Bolo*

Bosom Caresser Warming and sweet, for tender moments only.

½ oz madeira, ¼ oz brandy, ¼ oz curaçao, 1 teaspoon grenadine, 1 egg yolk.

Shake with ice, and strain into a cocktail glass.

Boston Cocktail A civilized New England apéritif.

1½ oz dry gin, 1 oz apricot brandy, 1 teaspoon lemon juice, a dash of grenadine.

Shake with ice, and strain into a cocktail glass.

Bourbon Cocktail Because of their sweet and fuller palate, American whiskeys are happier in cocktails than their sensitive European cousins, but they are not natural mixers. They marry best with flavours like peach and orange. This recipe is based loosely on David Embury's ideal bourbon cocktail.

2 oz bourbon, 1 oz lemon juice, $\frac{1}{3}$ oz curaçao, $\frac{1}{3}$ oz Bénédictine, 1 dash Angostura bitters.

Shake with cracked ice, and strain into a cocktail glass, or serve on the rocks in an Old Fashioned glass, decorated with a twist of lemon.

Bourbon Fog Although today there are few foggy days in London Town that is where this recipe came from, by the hand of John Doxat, a drinker of great distinction. In fact, it should clear the fog for all but the most misty late-night reveller. Serves fifteen to twenty.

1 quart bourbon, 1 quart well-chilled, very strong black coffee, 1 quart vanilla ice-cream.

Mix thoroughly in a punch bowl, and serve with a little ice in Old Fashioned or Collins glasses.

Brandied Ginger A delicious combination of treats for mid-afternoon or after dinner.

1 oz brandy, $\frac{1}{2}$ oz ginger brandy or ginger wine, 1 teaspoon (or more) lime juice, 1 teaspoon orange juice, 1 piece preserved ginger, grated chocolate.

Shake with ice cubes, strain into a cocktail glass, and decorate with the ginger, and/or dust with the chocolate.

Brandy Alexander An extravagant cocktail for an afternoon rendezvous. It is as toothsome as candy, but as seductive as surreptitious liquor.

1$\frac{1}{2}$ oz cognac or armagnac, 1 oz dark crème de cacao, 1 oz double cream, nutmeg.

Shake well with ice cubes, strain into a cocktail glass, dust with nutmeg.

Brave Bull Although its ingredients are from the Americas, this is a British recipe.

1 oz tequila, 1$\frac{1}{2}$ oz Kahlúa or Tia Maria.

Stir and pour over ice in an Old Fashioned glass.

★**Bronx** Probably one of the many cocktails that were devised to disguise bootleg gin from both the police and the palate during Prohibition. For a truly dry apéritif cocktail, forget the sweet vermouth. Use a blood orange for a Bloody Bronx; add an egg yolk for a sickly Golden Bronx.

1$\frac{1}{2}$ oz gin, $\frac{1}{2}$ oz dry vermouth, $\frac{1}{2}$ oz (or less) sweet vermouth, $\frac{1}{2}$ oz orange juice, $\frac{1}{2}$ oz lemon juice (optional).

Shake very briskly with ice cubes, strain into a wine glass, or serve on the rocks in an Old Fashioned glass.

The Buck Another product of Prohibition, in which
the distinguishing feature was the use of ginger
ale and lemon juice. A quarter of the lemon was
actually used as a garnish. The original Buck was
made with gin, like so many of the traditional
mixed drinks. While there is in most instances a
strong case for maintaining that tradition, there
is also much to be said for this unusual Brandy
Buck recipe. Why should gin have all the fun?
*1½ oz brandy, ½ oz lemon juice, ¾ oz crème de
menthe, ginger ale, a few seedless grapes.*
Shake all the ingredients except the ginger ale
with cracked ice. Serve on the rocks in a Collins
glass, top up with ginger ale, stir with a bar spoon,
and decorate with the grapes.

Buck's Fizz Neither a Buck nor a Fizz in the gin
sense, but a long, refreshing drink in which
champagne provides the uplift while the good-
ness of fresh orange juice cushions any subse-
quent falldown. Regency bucks knew what they
were doing. Serves four to six.
*1 bottle chilled champagne, 8 oz fresh orange
juice.*
Pour the orange juice into a pitcher, then add the
champagne. Decant into large, tall glasses.

Bullshot Authorities differ on the uses of this clever
and nutritious mixed drink. Trader Vic says it is
a good way to keep warm at a cold ball-game;
John Doxat recommends it for breakfast the
morning after; everyone agrees that it is a
relatively palatable "hair of the dog".
*2 oz vodka, 4 oz beef bouillon or 1 small can
condensed consommé, 1 bar spoon Worcestershire
sauce, a dash of Tabasco (optional), a dash of
cayenne pepper, salt to taste, the juice of ½ lemon,
1 lemon slice.*
Stir vigorously with plenty of ice, and strain into
an Old Fashioned glass, with a cube of ice and
the lemon slice.

Burgundy Cocktail The only recognized cocktail to
use burgundy as its basic ingredient. Warming
and sweet after-dinner drink.
*3 oz burgundy, 1 oz cognac, 3 to 4 drops
maraschino, 1 lemon slice or 1 cherry.*
Stir with ice cubes, strain into a cocktail glass,
and decorate with the lemon slice or cherry.

Byrrh Cocktail Despite the fact that it is pronounced
rather like "beer", the drink which gives its name
to this cocktail is a typically French apéritif. A
measure of Byrrh goes nicely with a slightly
smaller quantity of crème de cassis, ice and soda,

but bartenders like to marry it with a hard liquor, whether gin, bourbon or rye. The latter works best.

½ oz rye, ½ oz Byrrh, ½ oz dry French vermouth.

Shake with ice, and strain into a cocktail glass.

Café Amaretto A simple but delicious rich coffee ■ from the Souper, Aspen, Colorado. They call it Souper Coffee. Serve with Amaretti biscuits.

½ oz Amaretto, ½ oz Kahlúa (or Tia Maria) or quantities to taste, 1 cup scalding hot coffee, whipped cream.

Pour the liqueurs into the coffee and top with the whipped cream.

Café Brûlot There are many flaming coffees with a ■ variety of colourful names, and quite a few just called Café Brûlot. It is possible simply to float an ounce of cognac on top of a glass of hot coffee, and flame the liquor to great effect. The basic Brûlot is more of a punch, and this recipe can be embellished and varied to taste. Serves eight.

8 oz cognac, 1 pint scalding hot coffee, 2 sugar cubes, the peel of 1 lemon and 1 orange cut in a spiral, 8 cloves, 1 chopped vanilla bean, 2 to 3 sticks cinnamon.

Pour the brandy into a bowl, preferably made of silver. Add 1 sugar cube, the cloves, vanilla, cinnamon, orange and lemon peel. Stir well. Pour in the coffee. Soak the remaining cube of sugar in cognac, place it on a spoon, and light it. Dip the spoon containing the blazing cube into the coffee mixture, so that the flame spreads across the surface. Serve in small coffee cups.

Calisay Cocktail The excellent but slightly syrupy ☿ quinine liqueur of Catalonia is little used in cock- ♥ tails. This rare example is rather sweet, and can be given more after-dinner appeal with a slug of Spanish brandy.

1 oz Calisay, 1 oz sweet Italian vermouth, 3 dashes of sugar syrup, 3 dashes of lime juice.

Shake well with ice cubes, and strain into a cocktail glass.

Canadian Sunset Until this modern cocktail was ☿ devised, Canada lent its name only to a rather inappropriate rum-based drink and a Northern variation of the Old Fashioned.

2 oz Canadian whisky, 1 oz Galliano, 1 oz Strega, 2 oz lemon juice, 2 dashes Angostura bitters, 1 bar spoon grenadine.

Place the grenadine in a cocktail glass. Shake the remaining ingredients with ice cubes, and strain over the grenadine.

pe Codder This sustaining and refreshing drink
may be varied by the use of light rum or applejack as its base, and by the addition of soda,
2 oz vodka, juice of ½ lime, 4 oz cranberry juice.
Shake with ice, and serve on the rocks in a Collins
glass.

Carabinieri A cosmopolitan Canadian cocktail,
from Francisco Pedroche, of the Hyatt Regency
hotel, Toronto.
*¾ oz Galliano, 1 oz tequila, ½ oz Cointreau,
1 teaspoon Rose's lime juice, 3 oz orange juice,
1 egg yolk, 1 slice lime, 1 green and 1 red cherry.*
Shake thoroughly, and strain into a Collins glass
over crushed ice. Garnish with the lime slice and
cherries.

Caribbean Champagne A delicious sweet-and-dry
extravagance.
*4 oz dry champagne, ½ teaspoon white rum,
½ teaspoon banana liqueur, 1 to 2 dashes orange
bitters, 1 slice banana.*
Stir with crushed ice in a saucer-shaped champagne glass. Decorate with the banana slice.

Casablanca Bogey never sampled this recipe from
Japan, but it provides a rare opportunity to make
good use of advocaat.
*1 oz vodka, ½ oz (or fractionally more) advocaat,
1 teaspoon (or fractionally more) Galliano,
1 tablespoon lemon juice, 1 teaspoon orange juice.*
Shake and serve over crushed ice in a cocktail
glass, decorated with a thin slice of orange.

Chablis Cup An unusual refresher. Serves four.
*1 bottle chablis, 4 oz Grand Marnier, 4 oz kirsch,
2 to 3 peaches, 1 orange, cherries, 3 tablespoons
powdered sugar, mint sprigs.*
Peel and cut up the peaches, reserving any juice.
Slice the orange, and place with the cherries in a
small punch bowl. Pour on the chablis, and add
the powdered sugar. Stir gently, and refrigerate
for about 30 minutes. Garnish with sprigs of
mint, and serve in wine glasses.

★***Cherry Blossom*** Unquestionably a standard cocktail, and it comes in two versions, yet neither
works very well. Trader Vic says rather harshly,
"take your pick; they're both lousy." One version has nothing to do with cherries; it is made
with gin, raspberry syrup, orange bitters and egg
white. This is the other version.
*1 oz cherry brandy, 1 oz cognac, a few drops of
grenadine, a few drops of curaçao, ½ oz lemon
juice, sugar (optional).*
Shake very thoroughly with ice cubes (the drink

should be very cold), and strain into a cock...
glass which has been sugar-rimmed with che...
brandy.

Chicago Bomb The city's own drink should surely be
♈ made with bouillon. Instead, Chicago offers the
♥ choice of a rum fizz, a sort of champagne cocktail, and this rather sickly bomb.

*2 oz vanilla ice-cream, 1 teaspoon white crème de
cacao, 1 teaspoon green crème de menthe.*

Mix with cracked ice in an electric blender for a
few seconds at high speed. Serve straight up in a
cocktail glass.

★**Chinese Cocktail** Perhaps the rediscovery of China
♈ will lead us to a truly oriental cocktail. Until that
♥ happens, the best thing to drink before, during
and after a Chinese meal is either tea or heated
saké. The classic Chinese Cocktail has little to do
with the East.

*1½ oz Jamaica rum, 1 tablespoon grenadine, a few
dashes of curaçao, a few dashes of maraschino,
1 to 2 dashes Angostura bitters.*

Shake with cracked ice, and strain into a cocktail
glass.

Chocolate Cocktail A most unusual recipe from
♈ Harry Craddock, the godfather of all bartenders.
♥ *1 teaspoon grated dark chocolate, 1 egg yolk,
½ oz yellow Chartreuse, 1½ oz port.*

Shake thoroughly, and strain into a cocktail or
wine glass.

Cider Cup The west of England ciders are ferocious
🍺 enough to knock a man legless. Away from their
homeland, however, they are only found in a
tame condition which makes them fun at a party,
in punches, possets (hot, milky drinks) and
syllabubs (creamy desserts). Serves four.

*1 quart dry cider, 3 tablespoons brandy,
3 tablespoons Cointreau and/or maraschino, the
juice of 1 lemon, ½ pint fresh orange juice and/or
soda, orange and lemon slices.*

Thoroughly chill the cider. Mix it with the
remaining ingredients in a punch bowl, adding
the orange and lemon slices and ice at the last
minute. Serve in wine glasses.

★**The Claridge** An elegant early evening drink. It does
♈ not matter whether you are staying at Claridges
or just putting on the Ritz. Recipe from *The
Savoy Cocktail Book*.

*1 oz London Dry gin, 1 oz French dry vermouth,
½ oz Cointreau, ½ oz apricot brandy.*

Shake well with ice cubes, and strain into a cocktail glass.

Club An early classic which remains popular, and tops the list at Harry's Bar in the Park Lane Hotel, London.

1½ oz London Dry gin, ½ oz grenadine, juice of ½ lime, 1 egg white.

Shake with ice, and strain into a cocktail glass.

The Cobbler A style of mixed drink which is at least a century old. Cobblers are often made with wine (claret, Rhine wines, sauternes or fortified wine) instead of spirit as a base. The ingredients are neither stirred nor shaken before being poured into a large wine glass over crushed ice. Pour sugar or fruit syrup first, then liqueurs, then spirit or wine. Stir in the glass with a bar spoon, churning the ice until the drink has a frosted appearance. A Cobbler is decorated with seasonal fruits, and served with straws. The original may well be the Sherry Cobbler.

Ingredients in order of appearance:

1 teaspoon sugar syrup, a dash of grenadine, a dash of curaçao, 3 oz medium sherry.

Prepare and serve as above.

Coconut Shell Part of the fun comes from drinking out of the shell, of course, although coconut water is both delicious and nutritious. There are lots of coconut drinks, usually based on rum, but occasionally on brandy, or even bourbon. Complementary flavours include maraschino, almond and grapefruit.

3 oz light or golden rum, 1½ oz crème de banane, 2 large fresh coconuts.

Drain the coconuts, reserving the liquid. Scoop out the flesh, and mix it with the milk and other ingredients, with 3 to 4 oz crushed ice. Blend at high speed. If insufficiently liquid, add a little cream. Serve in the coconut shells.

Coconut Tequila A sweet and happy marriage.

1½ oz tequila, 2 teaspoons lemon juice, 2 teaspoons cream of coconut, 1 teaspoon maraschino.

Mix in a blender at low speed for 15 seconds, with crushed ice. Strain into a cocktail glass.

Coffee See *Café*

⋆***The Collins*** A rhyme from the 1890s refers to a John Collins who was a London barman. At that time, much of the gin produced there was still of the original Dutch type, which might explain why a John Collins was originally made with Hollands. The derivation of the Tom Collins may be just as simple. This version was originally made with sweetened gin, the best-known brand of which was Old Tom. Although Hollands gin is still readily available, and Old Tom continues to be produced in limited quantities, the two Collins are both commonly made with dry gin, and their names have become hopelessly confused. They have also been joined by Mike Collins (Irish whiskey), Jack (apple brandy) and such unlikely cousins as Pierre (cognac) and Pedro (rum). No doubt Juan (tequila) is lurking round the corner. A Collins is made with spirit, lemon and sugar. What distinguishes it most of all from the Sour is its size. A Collins is the tallest of mixed drinks, and is intended to be as refreshing as a lemonade, but with an added kick.

3 oz gin, the juice of 1 large lemon, 1 tablespoon (or less) sugar syrup, soda.

Pour ingredients into the tallest Collins glass you can find, add five large ice cubes and top up with soda. Stir thoroughly.

Cooch Behar An Indian recipe devised by a maharajah of Cooch Behar. If you cannot find pepper vodka (Okhotnichaya is a Russian brand), make your own. Steep a hot Mexican or Italian pepper in regular vodka for as long as you can wait, preferably a few weeks.

1½ oz pepper vodka, 3 oz tomato juice.

Shake thoroughly, and serve on the rocks in an Old Fashioned glass.

The Cooler A term rather vaguely used for other long, iced mixed drinks served in Collins glasses. A Cooler is dry, and may contain a couple of dashes of grenadine and a dash of bitters. Ginger ale may be used instead of soda. The ice may be cracked. David Embury decorates his Coolers with the peel of a whole lemon or orange, cut in a continuous spiral, curling over the edge of the glass, as in a Horse's Neck. This is the Sea Breeze Cooler.

1½ oz dry gin, 1½ oz apricot brandy (liqueur), the juice of ½ lemon, 2 dashes grenadine, soda, 2 or 3 fresh sprigs of mint.

Prepare as for Collins. Decorate with the mint.

Corpse Reviver The name has clearly caught the imagination of many barmen, for there are at least three well-established varieties of Corpse Reviver, each intended to be a well-bred hair of the dog. Endless variations, not to mention Sally Bowles' toothpaste "oyster".

1. 1 oz cognac, 1 oz Fernet Branca, 1 oz white crème de menthe or peppermint schnapps.

2. 2 oz cognac, 1 oz calvados or applejack, 1 oz sweet Italian vermouth.

   3. 1oz dry gin, 1oz Cointreau, 1oz China-Martini or Swedish Punsch, 1oz lemon juice, a dash of Pernod.

In each case, retire to a sound-proof room while someone else shakes the mixture very thoroughly before straining into a cocktail glass.

The Crusta An elaborate version of the Sour, best
Ⴘ served in a wine glass, and most often made with brandy.

   2oz brandy, ½oz lemon juice, 1 teaspoon maraschino, 1 teaspoon curaçao (optional), 2 dashes bitters, the peel of 1 lemon (or orange), cut in a continuous spiral.

Line the glass with the peel. Moisten the edge of the glass, and dip in sugar, to frost the rim and the upper edge of the peel. Shake the ingredients with crushed ice, and strain into the glass.

★*Cuba Libre* It is not quite clear who liberated what
◼ from whom, except that the Bacardi company left Cuba for Puerto Rico. After all their efforts, one authority recommends Philippine rum, which hardly seems appropriate. A miniature version is sometimes made for the cocktail glass, and the whole thing can be reformulated with Southern Comfort.

   1 lime, 2oz Bacardi or other light rum, Coca-Cola.

Squeeze the lime into a Collins glass, and drop in the lime shells. Pound them with a bar spoon. Fill the glass with large ice cubes. Add rum, then top up with coke. Stir lightly but thoroughly.

The Cup A wine-based summer drink mixed in quan-
◼ tity. See ***Cider Cup*** and ***Chablis Cup***. The Coronation Crystal Cup is unusual in that it employs marsala, a fortified wine often confined to the kitchen. Serves four to six.

   3 glasses marsala or madeira, 1 bottle inexpensive white wine, ½ lemon, 1 pint (or more) soda, borage.

Slice the ½ lemon, and mix with all the ingredients except the soda, in a jug or bowl, with chunks of ice. Refrigerate for at least 2 hours. Add soda just before serving, and stir gently. The leaf of the borage plant adds an agreeable cucumberish flavour to a summer cup, and the flower is a pleasant floating decoration.

★*Daiquiri* Although this name was briefly adopted as
Ⴘ a brand by a rum-distiller, it properly belongs to a classic cocktail made famous by Constante Ribalagua of La Florida restaurant, Havana, in the first half of the twentieth century. He had five recipes, and there are countless others, but

Daiquiri drinkers are notoriously fussy about the end result. David Embury emphasizes the importance of using lime juice, not lemon juice, although some recipes add a teaspoon of the latter, or of orange, grapefruit or pineapple juice. Embury also cautions against allowing the oil from the peel to enter the drink (it spoils a Daiquiri but makes a Martini). Trader Vic speaks highly of Barbados rum, although, in the absence of Cuban, Puerto Rican is most commonly used. Variations include the use of two dashes of grenadine, curaçao, apricot brandy, or pineapple liqueur.

1½–2 oz light rum, juice of ½ lime, 1 dash sugar syrup or 1 teaspoon powdered sugar, 1 dash maraschino (optional).

There are two styles of preparation. The mixture can be shaken very thoroughly with plenty of crushed ice, and strained into a cocktail glass. Or it can be mixed with the ice in a blender, piled up in a champagne glass, and served with a short straw. Although the ingredients and proportions vary in different recipes, the predominant tastes should be lime and rum, and the drink should taste dry and smooth. The frozen version should have the consistency of a lightly frozen water-ice.

The Daisy A drink of the Sour type which contains either raspberry syrup or grenadine and is customarily served in a metal tankard full of crushed ice, with straws. The original Daisy may have been made with gin, and many recipes use rum, but bourbon arguably works best.

1½ oz bourbon, 1 oz raspberry juice, the juice of ½ lemon, ½ teaspoon sugar, soda, raspberries, 1 orange slice.

Shake with ice cubes, and strain over crushed ice in a metal tankard. Top up with soda. Stir thoroughly with a bar spoon until the tankard becomes very cold. Decorate with raspberries and the orange slice.

Danish Gin Fizz The Scandinavian element is the Cherry Heering. This distinctively dry cherry brandy is still made by the family of Peter Heering near Copenhagen.

1½ oz gin, ½ oz Cherry Heering, 1 teaspoon kirschwasser, 2 teaspoons lime juice, 1½ teaspoons sugar syrup.

Shake vigorously for some minutes with crushed ice, and strain into a chilled Highball glass. Aggressively top up with plenty of soda, and drink before it stops fizzing.

Danny's Special A good bourbon drink, but why not Jack Daniel's?

2 oz whiskey, 1 oz Cointreau, 1 teaspoon Grand Marnier, 3 tablespoons lemon juice.

Stir, and serve in an Old Fashioned glass.

Diablo A rare opportunity to use white port. A quite different recipe is based on tequila, cassis, lime and ginger.

1½ oz dry white port, 1 oz sweet vermouth, a few drops lemon juice.

Shake with ice, and strain into a cocktail glass.

Diabolo The addition of one vowel changes Diablo into a rum recipe, from England.

2 oz rum, ½ oz Cointreau, ½ oz dry vermouth, 2 drops Angostura bitters, orange peel.

Shake with crushed ice, and serve with a little crushed ice in a cocktail glass. Garnish with a twist of orange peel.

Dry Martini The finest of all cocktails. Subtle, potent and a wonderful apéritif, it even has good looks. This single cocktail inspired a whole book, *Stirred—Not Shaken*, by John Doxat. He believes that the drink was invented for John D. Rockefeller by a bartender, whose name was Martini, at the Knickerbocker Hotel, New York City, in about 1910. It was originally made with French vermouth, and only later did the dry vermouth from Martini and Rossi of Italy become a favourite ingredient. How much vermouth? Doxat talks of one barman who allegedly is content just to let the shadow of the vermouth bottle fall across the gin. Another considers it sufficient merely to bow in the direction of France while stirring the gin and ice. The essence of a Martini is its dryness. Doxat pours 4 oz of vermouth (Martini Extra Dry) into a mixing glass half-filled with large ice cubes. As soon as the vermouth reaches the bottom of the glass, he pours it off and discards it. He then pours in at least 2 oz of High and Dry gin per serving, and stirs very briskly for about 30 seconds before straining into chilled glasses. He believes enough vermouth clings to the ice to produce a ratio of 1:11 against the gin. Doxat argues that the highest acceptable proportion of vermouth to gin is 1:7, which David Embury believes to be perfect. Mixes of 1:15 and more have been known to produce excellent cocktails, and people have attempted to pass off as Martinis drinks made at 1:2.

Which gin? Most Martinians like their drink, in its shivering splendour, to look almost colourless; Embury admires the golden hue imparted by the gin which is labelled simply, Booth's. Lesser bars and supermarkets may have cut-price gins that are made to a lower alcohol content, and in some brands the botanicals are infused rather than distilled; a good Martini requires plenty of alcohol and a clean, subtle, full flavour. Beefeater, Bombay and Tanqueray score on dryness; Gordon's scores on full flavour.

The coldness of the cocktail is also important. This can be intensified by a longer period of stirring, or Bondian shaking, but that damages by dilution. On the grounds of both appearance and dilution, a Martini on the rocks is not quite the same thing. Nor is a "Vodkatini".

The last essential is to cut a sliver of rind from a lemon, and squeeze it, skin side down, over the drink. A just-visible, fine spray of oil called the zest is thus directed on to the surface of the drink. Do not float the rind, or decorate with an olive, unless you want a slightly oilier finish. Olives, if used, must in no circumstances be stuffed. A dash of orange bitters adds to the subtlety of the cocktail, but its drying effect has been used to disguise an unhealthily low proportion of gin.

1 whisper dry vermouth, 1 avalanche London Dry gin, a touch of orange bitters (optional), lemon zest.

Stir the vermouth, gin and orange bitters in a mixing glass amid a mountain of ice cubes, for a maximum of 30 seconds. Strain into a chilled Martini glass. Squeeze on lemon zest. Ask any drinking guests whether decorations are to be worn.

★*Diana* Pretty, feminine, sweet, and delightful after dinner.
♥ *2 oz white crème de menthe or peppermint schnapps, 2 to 3 teaspoons cognac.*
Pack a small wine glass with crushed ice, and pour in the crème de menthe. Float the brandy on top by pouring it gently over an inverted teaspoon.

★*Doctor* Several recipes, all based on Swedish punsch, with citrus juice and perhaps another spirit.
1 oz Swedish punsch, 1 oz vodka (a case for Finlandia?), 1 oz orange juice, 1 oz lemon juice.
Shake with ice cubes, and serve on the rocks in an Old Fashioned glass.

Dolores An opportunity to use Spanish brandy in a mixed drink. A quite different Dolores is made with Jamaica rum, dry sherry and Dubonnet.

$\frac{3}{4}$ *oz Spanish brandy,* $\frac{3}{4}$ *oz cherry brandy,* $\frac{3}{4}$ *oz crème de cacao.*

Shake with ice, and strain into a cocktail glass. Decorate with a cherry on a cocktail stick.

Dubonnet Cassis A delightfully refreshing, very French apéritif for a sunny evening.

2 oz red Dubonnet, 1 oz crème de cassis, Perrier.

Stir briskly in a large wine glass or Old Fashioned glass, with a large cube of ice. Top up with Perrier.

Durango A tequila drink in · which Calistoga spring water, from California, is specified by the *Complete World Bartender Gŭide*. Although no two spring waters are the same, Calistoga shares some properties of the most famous European examples, notably a fairly high calcium content. The spring is hot, the water—unlike Perrier—is artificially carbonated.

1$\frac{1}{2}$ oz tequila, 1$\frac{1}{2}$ oz concentrated frozen grapefruit juice (undiluted), 1 teaspoon orgeat syrup or a bar spoon of almond extract, spring water, mint sprigs.

Shake with cracked ice, strain over ice cubes into an Old Fashioned or Collins glass. Top up with spring water. Garnish with mint sprigs.

Dutch Trade Winds The island of Curaçao, famous for its green oranges, was colonized by the Dutch. Hence the name of this excellent cocktail. The Dutch like their glasses filled to the brim, and bend over the bar to sip the first taste without touching the glass. If your glass is not brimful, add some more gin. Although there are many brands of Dutch gin and liqueurs, the most readily available outside The Netherlands is Bols.

2 oz Dutch jenever gin (Claeryn, if you can find it), $\frac{1}{2}$ *oz Dutch curaçao,* $\frac{1}{2}$ *oz lemon juice, sugar syrup to taste.*

Shake thoroughly with cracked ice, and strain into a cocktail glass.

Earthquake A fun drink with tequila, or an insane mixture which is guaranteed to induce inner tremors.

1. *1$\frac{1}{2}$ oz tequila, 1 teaspoon grenadine, 2 dashes orange bitters (or Cointreau, if you prefer it sweeter), 2 strawberries, 1 orange slice.*

Mix in a blender at high speed for 15 seconds, with 3 oz crushed ice. Strain into a cocktail glass, and decorate with the strawberries and the orange slice.

2. $\frac{1}{2}$ *oz gin,* $\frac{1}{2}$ *oz bourbon,* $\frac{1}{2}$ *oz Pernod.*

Shake with ice, and strain into a cocktail glass.

★*East India* Shouldn't it be West Indies? Variations
🍸 may be made with maraschino and raspberry
♥ syrup.
*1½ oz brandy, ¼ oz curaçao, ¼ oz pineapple juice,
a dash Angostura bitters.*
Shake with ice, and strain into a cocktail glass.

★*East Indian* Variations may be made by including
🍸 peach bitters, a dash of maraschino, and a mint
garnish.
*1½ oz dry sherry, 1½ oz dry vermouth, 2 dashes
orange bitters.*
Shake with ice, and strain into a cocktail glass.

Egg Nog Nashville Country-style seems to take a
🍺 leaf out of Mrs Beeton's book. Serves about
twenty-five.
*1 pint brandy, 1 pint Jamaica rum, 1 quart
bourbon, 18 eggs, 3 quarts heavy (double)
cream, 1 lb sugar, cloves, nutmegs.*
Stir the liquors with the egg yolks. Mix the cream
and sugar, and blend into the liquor mixture.
Beat the egg whites until stiff, and fold them in
gently. Garnish with cloves and nutmeg. Serve in
mugs.

★*El Presidente* A distant relation of the Daiquiri.
🍸 *1½ oz light rum, ½ oz curaçao (optional), ½ oz
French dry vermouth, 2 dashes grenadine.*
Stir or shake with ice cubes, and strain into a
cocktail glass.

Eldorado A honey-and-vitamin drink for health-
🍺 food freaks who like an alcoholic kick.
*1 tablespoon honey, 1½ oz lemon juice, 2 oz
tequila, 1 orange slice.*
Shake well with cracked ice, and strain over rocks
in a Collins glass. Decorate with the orange slice.

Emerald Sometimes called Emerald Isle or Star.
🍸 There are all sorts of variations, including one
satanic recipe which threatens the drinker with
rum, gin, apricot brandy, curaçao and lemon
juice, all in one glass. Surely green crème de
menthe must feature? In one version it is blended
in equal parts with brandy, and sometimes,
diabolically, cayenne is added. The following
cocktail is also known as the Erin. See also
Everybody's Irish.
*2–3 oz Cork gin, 1 teaspoon green crème de
menthe, a few dashes of green Pomeranz or
Angostura bitters, 1 green cherry.* Optional
extras: *lemon juice, egg white, even nutmeg,* but
end result must be indisputably emerald.
Shake with cracked ice, and strain into a cocktail
112 glass. Decorate with the cherry.

English Bishop See *Bishop*

English Bolo A stateless Bolo is a rather ordinary drink made with rum and fruit juices. An English one is a sherry oddity with something of a Christmas feel.

4 oz dry sherry, 1½ oz lemon juice, 1 teaspoon sugar, 1 cinnamon stick.

Pound the cinnamon with the lemon juice and sugar in an Old Fashioned glass. Add the sherry, and stir.

English Shrub See *The Shrub*

Eton Blazer A metaphorical name, no doubt, since Eton College does not have a blazer. Nor is the college's colour, black, evident in this drink. Not a Blazer in the Blue sense.

2 oz gin, ½ oz kirsch, juice of ½ lemon, 1–2 teaspoons sugar, soda.

Shake well with ice cubes, and serve with 2 or 3 ice cubes in a Collins glass. Top up with soda.

Everybody's Irish The green olive suspended in the drink "looks like a gibbous moon", according to Harry Craddock.

1½ oz Irish whiskey, 1 teaspoon green Chartreuse, 2 dashes of green crème de menthe, 1 green olive.

Stir with ice, strain into a cocktail glass, and add the olive.

Fancy Free An excellent rye cocktail.

1½ oz rye, 2 dashes maraschino, a dash of orange bitters, a dash of Angostura bitters.

Dip the rim of a cocktail glass into lemon juice and powdered sugar. Shake the drink with ice cubes, and strain into the glass.

Fernet Cocktail Taken as a "digestif" in Italy and France, and as a hangover cure in other countries, Fernet and Fernet-Branca (two different brands) still manage to find their way into the odd mixed drink. If you are feeling delicate, try a highball made with 1 part grenadine to 3 parts Fernet, and no whiskey. As a digestif, try the following recipe.

1½ oz cognac, 1½ oz Fernet, 1 teaspoon sugar, orange peel.

Stir with lots of ice, and strain into a cocktail glass. Squeeze a sliver of orange peel over each glass, and use as decoration.

Fifth Avenue A colourful and pretty drink, according to *The Savoy Cocktail Book*, but a less interesting cocktail of Fernet, gin and vermouth if everyone else is to be believed.

1 oz dark crème de cacao, 1 oz apricot brandy, 1 oz sweetened cream.

113

Use narrow liqueur or Pousse-café glass. Pour the ingredients in gently and slowly so that they stand in layers without mixing.

Fino Martini An almost acceptable variation on the
☿ great cocktail, although one authority's half-and-half mix makes this less than a Martini.

2oz London Dry gin, 1 teaspoon fino sherry.

Prepare and serve as for Dry Martini.

The Fix A pineapple version of The Daisy, served in
∎ a Highball glass. That is the most clear-cut
♥ definition, although there is bored confusion about the distinction between these two Victorian categories of mixed drink. The truth is surely lost in the alcoholic mists of time.

2oz London Dry gin, ¼oz pineapple syrup, ¼oz lime juice, ¼oz lemon juice, a dash of Cointreau, lemon rind, fresh pineapple pieces.

Shake with crushed ice, and serve with a straw in a Highball glass. Put a substantial piece of lemon rind in the glass, and decorate with the pineapple.

★**The Fizz** A drink bearing this name should fizz. In
∎ order to achieve this, it may be necessary to shake the mixture for several minutes (with crushed ice), or to use a blender. It is certainly essential to employ the soda siphon with some gusto; a bottle of soda will not do. The Fizz is really a form of seltzer for the person who cannot face a drink after last night. It should be drunk at about 11.30 in the morning, before the pre-lunch cocktail. The basic fizz is made with gin, although all the other hard liquors have muscled in. Two sprigs of mint convert it into an Alabama Fizz; in a Texan version the juice of an orange quarter and a lemon quarter is added. There is much to be said for the addition of an egg white, which makes it into Silver Fizz. There is also a Golden Fizz, using egg yolk, but only the very sick or very healthy can take it. See also **Ramos Fizz**.

2oz gin, 1oz (or more) lemon juice, 1oz (or less) sugar, soda.

Shake with crushed ice, and strain into a Highball glass, straight up. Attack with soda, while simultaneously stirring. Drink immediately, while the fizzing continues.

Fjord The aquavit should ideally be from Norway,
☿ since that is where the fjords are.
♥ *2 teaspoons Norwegian Linie aquavit, 1oz brandy, 2 teaspoons orange juice, 2 teaspoons lime juice, 1 teaspoon grenadine.*

Shake well with ice, and strain on to ice cubes in an Old Fashioned glass.

114

Jersey As if that unloved state has ... enough already. Serves about ...

... art apple brandy, 8 oz sugar, a few dashes ... ostura bitters.

Warm the brandy, and mix it with the sugar and bitters in a punch bowl, until completely blended. Ignite the mixture at the table, and extinguish with a large kettle of boiling water. Stir, and serve hot in mugs.

Flaming Glögg The floating torch is the fun part. Serves about ten.

1½ pints aquavit, 1 bottle red wine, 1 cup orange juice, cardamom seeds, ginger root, whole cloves, 1 cinnamon stick, dried fruits, grated citrus rind, sugar to taste, ½ grapefruit.

Reserve 1 cup aquavit, and mix all the other ingredients in a saucepan. Simmer thoroughly without boiling. Serve in a chafing dish. To make the floating torch, scoop the flesh out of the grapefruit half, moisten the rim and inside of the grapefruit shell with aquavit and press it in sugar. Float the shell on the glögg, fill it with the reserved aquavit until it is overflowing, and light the spirit. Let it burn for a few minutes, then overturn the shell into the glögg.

Florida Made with orange juice, of course. There are several variations, including a quite different recipe with pineapple juice and lime juice, rum and crème de menthe.

1¼ oz orange juice, ½ oz gin, 1 teaspoon kirschwasser, 1 teaspoon triple sec, 1 teaspoon lemon juice.

Shake well with ice cubes, and serve on the rocks in a Collins glass.

Flying Dutchman The Netherlands' answer to the Dry Martini.

3 oz ice-cold jenever gin, 1 teaspoon Dutch curaçao, a dash of orange bitters.

Put the curaçao into a chilled glass and swirl round. Empty the glass. Pour in the gin.

Flying Scotsman Would any Scot drink this?

1½ oz scotch, 1½ oz sweet vermouth, a dash of sugar syrup, a dash of Angostura bitters.

Stir well with ice, and strain into a cocktail glass.

Fraises Fizz An unusual variation on the Gin Fizz. The bartender who devised this favoured the fraises (strawberry liqueur) from Chambéry.

1½ oz gin, 1 oz strawberry liqueur, 2 teaspoons lemon juice, 1½ teaspoons sugar syrup, 1 twist lemon peel, 1 strawberry.

Shake well with crushed ice,
Highball glass, straight up.
vigorously. Decorate with the le
strawberry.

French Sherbert An indulgent luxury for l♥vers
Somehow suited to well-appointed hotel rooms
¼ oz cognac, ¼ oz kirsch, 1 teaspoon sugar,
Angostura bitters to taste, champagne,
cherry water-ice or flavour of your choice.
Stir all but the last two ingredients in a Collin
glass. Top up the glass part way with champagne
then float a small scoop of water-ice. Drench the
water-ice in champagne.

French Green Dragon A ritzy after-dinner drink.
♈ 1½ oz cognac, 1½ oz green Chartreuse.
Shake well with crushed ice, and strain into a
cocktail glass.

Frisco Sour An excellent whiskey cocktail, using
♈ Bénédictine instead of sugar.
2–3 oz rye, 1 oz Bénédictine, ¼ oz lemon juice,
¼ oz fresh lime juice.
Shake with cracked ice, and strain into a Sour
glass.

Frozen Berkeley Many other frozen drinks, using a
♈ variety of fruits (apples, bananas, berry fruits)
♥ and different spirit bases (aquavit, tequila, brandies) can be made by the same method.
½ oz California brandy, 2 teaspoons passion-fruit
juice, 1½ oz light rum.
Mix in a blender with 3 oz crushed ice at low
speed for no more than 15 seconds. Strain
straight up into a cocktail or champagne glass.

Gaelic Coffee See **Irish Coffee**

Genoa A chance to get out the sambuca. In one
♈ recipe equal parts of grappa and gin are used.
Although juniper is grown in Italy, it doesn't
really suit this drink.
2 teaspoons sambuca, 2 teaspoons Martini dry
vermouth, 1½ oz grappa (Bosso Vecchio, if
possible). If grappa is unavailable, use marc,
or Italian brandy.
Shake with ice, and serve with 2 to 3 ice cubes in
an Old Fashioned glass. Or shake without ice,
and serve in a brandy snifter.

German Band Probably a Chicagoan confection, al-
♈ though the name is Cockney rhyming slang for
"hand".
2 oz (or more) Steinhäger schnapps, ¼ oz (or
less) kirschwasser or blackberry liqueur
(preferably Echte Kroatzbeere), a dash of
Underberg or Kabänes bitters.

einhäger. Stir the in- ... a mixing glass, and ... ith no decoration. ... with two cocktail ... ten thought. This drink is suppos... ...oast to the well-endowed Gibson Girls.

Ingredients and method as for Dry Martini.

Gimlet There is widespread disagreement over the proportions, but the Gimlet is generally agreed to be a short gin and lime drink, while a Rickey is a medium or long one.

1½ oz London Dry or Plymouth gin, ½ oz Rose's lime juice.

Shake with ice, and strain into a cocktail glass.

Gin Fizz See *The Fizz*

Gin Rickey See *The Rickey*

Gin Sling See *The Sling*

Gin and French Smart but simple cocktail which predates the Dry Martini. There is none of the ritual, just gin and French dry vermouth poured straight into a cocktail glass, with ice very optional. Proportions 1:1, or whatever suits you. The same drink with sweet vermouth is Gin and It(alian).

Ginger Highball Instead of using dry ginger, impress your guests with a little culinary care.

2 oz bourbon, 1 large piece fresh ginger root, soda.

Pour the whiskey into a Highball glass. Squeeze the ginger on to the liquor with a garlic press. Add 2 to 3 ice cubes, and stir gently. Add soda.

Ginger Rum Tea This drink can be taken hot, or it can be chilled.

1½ oz rum, 1 cup hot tea, 1 piece preserved ginger.

Pour the rum into the tea, add the ginger and stir.

Glögg A hot wine drink in which dried fruits such as raisins and figs are used (see *Flaming Glögg*). Other typical ingredients are blanched almonds and cardamom seeds.

Gloom Chaser There is great confusion about both the name (see also *Gloom Raiser* and *Gloom Lifter*) and the ingredients. The basic recipe was probably Harry Craddock's. Other people add gin, dry vermouth, and sweet vermouth.

¾ oz curaçao, ¾ oz Grand Marnier, ¾ oz grenadine, ¾ oz lemon juice.

Shake well with cracked ice, and strain into a cocktail glass.

Gloom Lifter This is probably a more efficacious mixture. In one recipe a teaspoon of brandy is added for no good reason.

117

2oz Irish whiskey, ½oz (or slightly ..
juice, ¼oz sugar syrup, ½ an egg white.
Shake with ice, and strain into a cocktail

Gloom Raiser In this instance, does raise mean disp
or produce? No doubt the former was the inter
tion of its creator, "Robert", of Riviera an
R.A.C. Club fame. Yet, whatever it did to Lor
don clubmen during World War I, it is
depressing way to treat a Dry Martini.
2oz (or a little more) London Dry gin, ¼oz (or
much less) French dry vermouth, 2 dashes
Pernod, 2 dashes grenadine (optional).
Prepare and serve as for a Dry Martini.

Glühwein In German, "glowing wine". See **Mullec**
Wine

Golden Cadillac Instead of the cacao, use Cointreau,
with ½oz orange juice, and you have a Golden
Dream.
1oz Galliano, ½oz white crème de cacao, ½oz
double cream.
Shake well with ice cubes, and strain into a cocktail glass.

Golf Cocktail A Dry Martini with too much vermouth, and Angostura bitters. Use the excellent
Lillet vermouth instead, and it becomes a Great
Secret.
2oz London Dry gin, 1 teaspoon dry vermouth,
1 to 2 dashes Angostura bitters.
Prepare and serve as Dry Martini.

Grand Quetsch A chance to use the superb white, dry
brandy of the Switzen plum.
1oz Grand Marnier, 1 teaspoon quetsch, 1
teaspoon orange juice, 1 orange slice.
Stir without ice. Pour over crushed ice into a
cocktail or champagne glass. Decorate with the
orange slice.

Grand Passion In the traditional recipe gin is used,
but white rum or tequila works better.
1½oz gin, 1oz passion-fruit juice (or ¼oz
passion-fruit liqueur), 1 to 2 dashes of Angostura
or peach bitters.
Shake well with crushed ice, and strain into a
cocktail glass.

Grappa Strega An all-Italian after-dinner drink for
lovers.
1oz grappa, 1oz Strega, 1 teaspoon lemon juice,
1 teaspoon orange juice.
Shake with ice, and serve in a cocktail glass.

Greek Buck To accompany a mid-afternoon honey
cake, some Greek Delight, a gritty coffee and a
game of backgammon.

$1\frac{1}{2}$ oz Metaxa brandy, 1 teaspoon ouzo,
2 teaspoons lemon juice, ginger ale.

Shake the brandy and lemon juice with ice cubes, and strain on to ice cubes in a Collins glass. Pour on ginger ale and float the ouzo on top.

Green Dragon One fire-breathing recipe includes gin, kümmel, crème de menthe, lemon juice and peach bitters. Even dragons can be more civilized than that.

2 oz Pernod, 2 oz milk, 2 oz (or less) double cream, 1 oz (or less) sugar syrup.

Shake with ice cubes, and strain into a chilled *ballon* wine glass over plenty of rocks.

Green Lady A recipe from France.

$\frac{1}{2}$ oz green Chartreuse, $\frac{1}{2}$ oz yellow Chartreuse, $\frac{1}{4}$ oz lime juice, $1\frac{1}{2}$ oz London Dry gin (preferably Boodles), 1 sliver of lime.

Shake with crushed ice, and strain into a cocktail glass. Decorate with the lime sliver.

Green Mist A recipe from Denmark. It is better without the sweet vermouth, and with fractionally more Galliano.

$\frac{3}{4}$ oz Galliano, $\frac{3}{4}$ oz green Chartreuse, $\frac{3}{4}$ oz Italian dry vermouth, $\frac{3}{4}$ oz Italian sweet vermouth.

Stir with ice cubes and strain into a cocktail glass.

Grog A most useful antidote for when a hot summer afternoon suddenly turns into a chilly evening. There are endless variations on the recipe.

2 oz Jamaica rum, 1 tablespoon lemon juice, 1 sugar cube, 6 cloves, 1 cinnamon stick, 1 slice lemon.

Mix in a heatproof mug with boiling water. Stir to dissolve the sugar, and add the lemon slice.

Harvey Wallbanger The story is that Harvey was a Californian surfer. After losing an important contest, he consoled himself excessively with his favourite drink, a Screwdriver with a dash of Galliano. As he left the bar, he staggered and bounced from one wall to the other. Harvey Wallbanger, they called him.

2 oz vodka, 1 teaspoon to 2 tablespoons Galliano, orange juice, $\frac{1}{2}$ teaspoon sugar (very optional).

Shake the vodka, orange juice and sugar, if used, with ice cubes. Pour over ice cubes into a Collins or Old Fashioned glass, or strain into a cocktail glass. Float the Galliano on top.

Hemingway Drink three or five of these slowly, said Hemingway, when he offered this recipe to *Esquire*. He mockingly called it Death in the Afternoon.

$1\frac{1}{2}$ oz absinthe (Pernod), chilled champagne.

Pour the Pernod into a champagne glass. Add champagne until it attains the proper opalescent milkiness.

★ ***The Highball*** It is said that some American railroad used a signal with a ball raised on a pole to indicate to the train driver that he was running late. A highball meant "hurry". It also came to mean a simple drink that could be fixed in a hurry. The Highball has no precise definition, but it is generally agreed to mean a 1½-oz jigger of American whiskey over 1 or 2 large cubes of ice in a straight 6 to 8 oz glass, topped up with soda, and given a light stir.

Honolulu Cocktail Two recipes from Trader Vic.

 ⅞ *1. 1½oz gin, 1 dash bitters, ¼ teaspoon orange juice, ¼ teaspoon pineapple juice, ¼ teaspoon lemon juice, ½ teaspoon powdered sugar.*
 Shake well with ice cubes, and strain into a chilled cocktail glass.

 ♥ *2. ¾oz gin, ¾oz maraschino, ¾oz Bénédictine.*
 Stir well with ice cubes, and strain into a chilled cocktail glass.

★ ***Horse's Neck*** A plain Horse's Neck contains no alcohol, but a kick is normally added by using whiskey, or sometimes gin.
 2½ oz bourbon or rye, ginger ale, the peel of lemon, cut in a continuous spiral.
 Place the lemon peel inside a Collins glass, so that it curls over the edge. Put 4 large cubes of ice in the glass. Pour in the whiskey, and top up with ginger ale.

★ ***Hot Buttered Rum*** The easy method is to make a hot drink with rum and spiced cider, and to stir a pat of butter into each mug. The great exponent of this drink, Trader Vic, makes a "batter" first. In *Trader Vic's Bartender Guide*, he refers to it as "our famous formula".
 1½ oz light Puerto Rican rum, 1 lb brown sugar, ¼lb softened butter, ¼–½ teaspoon ground nutmeg, ¼–½ teaspoon ground cinnamon, ¼–½ teaspoon ground cloves, a pinch of salt, 1 eight-inch cinnamon stick.
 Beat the sugar and butter together until they are thoroughly creamed and fluffy. Beat in the nutmeg, cinnamon, cloves and salt. Put a heaped teaspoon of this "batter" in each mug. Add the rum, top up with hot water, stir well, and mull with a hot poker. Decorate with the cinnamon stick.

Hot Rum Cow Milky alcoholic drinks seem to have become known as Cows. This one is another of Trader Vic's variations.

1 teaspoon powdered sugar, 1 dash Angostura
bitters, 1 dash vanilla essence, 8 oz very hot milk,
1½ oz light Puerto Rican rum, grated nutmeg.

Mix thoroughly in a blender. Pour into a large
heated mug. Dust with nutmeg.

ceberg Nearly all liqueurs are delicious with ice-
cream or water-ice. Strega flavours a famous
Italian ice-cream, and here its rival Galliano suf-
fuses a water-ice.

1 oz Galliano, 2 teaspoons Cointreau, 2 oz orange
water-ice.

Mix in blender until smooth, and serve in a stemmed narrow glass (Parfait, or Pousse-café), with
a straw.

cebreaker In one recipe this name is bestowed upon
a rum-laced tea; in another it is given to a
Daiquirish tequila drink.

2 oz tequila, 2 oz grapefruit juice, 1 tablespoon
grenadine, 2 teaspoons Cointreau, 4 oz crushed
ice.

Mix in blender at low speed for 15 seconds, and
strain into a Sour glass straight up.

ced Coffee Fillip Many liqueurs make delicious
additions to iced coffee. Try also crème de cacao,
kirsch, or crème de menthe. For a kick with a
flavour, use Jamaica rum or Irish whiskey.

8 oz very strong black coffee, 2 teaspoons Tia
Maria or Kahlúa.

Stir thoroughly, and chill until ice-cold.

ndependence Day Punch What to drink on July 4?
One answer is 2 quarts bourbon, mixed with
1 pint pineapple juice, 8 oz lime juice, and soda.
The following response is more elaborate. Serves
fifteen.

1 bottle chilled champagne, 1 bottle cognac,
3 bottles dry red wine, 1 pint strong tea, the juice
of 2 dozen lemons, 2 lb powdered sugar, lemon
slices.

Dissolve the sugar in the lemon juice in a large
punch bowl. Add the tea, and large chunks of ice,
then the wine and cognac. Chill thoroughly. Immediately before serving, pour in the champagne.
Serve in wine goblets. Decorate with the lemon
slices.

rish Coffee Although Irish whiskey is a wonderful
spirit in its own right, its worldwide reputation is
owed to the invention of Gaelic Coffee. Today,
every other spirit is used in hot coffee drinks, but
none works better than Irish. This case is put
concisely by Brian Murphy, an Englishman
despite his name, in his *World Book of Whisky*:

"Some magic in the flavours of coffee and Iris whiskey produces a taste quite different fro either, but within which you can still distinguis the original elements." In the days when tran atlantic aeroplanes had to stop for fuel at Sha non, the weather in the wild west of Ireland wa fought with Gaelic Coffee in the airport ba whence the habit spread to the United States. Th great authority Grossman supports the claim the Buena Vista Café, Fisherman's Wharf, Sa Francisco, to have pioneered Irish Coffee in th Americas, although doubtless there are man other contenders.

1 teaspoon sugar, 1½ oz Irish whiskey, 5 oz very strong, scalding-hot black coffee made from freshly ground beans, heavy (double) cream.

Rinse an 8 oz stemmed goblet with hot wate Place the sugar in the glass, followed by th whiskey. Add the coffee, leaving enough roon for the cream. Stir thoroughly, and wait until th surface is calm before adding the cream by pour ing it very slowly over the back of a teaspoon The cream must float on top of the coffee, and no blend into the drink. If you fail, don't serve th drink to your guests; knock it back quickly your self, and try again.

Irish Cow The double-cream, chocolate-flavoure whiskey made by Bailey's of Dublin, makes superb nightcap in a hot milk drink. Proportion to taste.

★*Jack Rose* The best-known applejack drink, very similar to the Rabbit.

2 oz apple brandy, the juice of 1 lime (or less), a dash of grenadine (or more).

Shake with ice, and strain into a cocktail glass.

Jackie O's Rose Same principle as Jack, bu different ingredients. It may need sweetening with sugar.

2 oz light rum, ½ oz lime juice, a dash of Cointreau, sugar to taste.

Serve as Jack, or over crushed ice in a Sour glass.

Jamaica Ginger Beer This is worth the trouble. Gin ger beer is altogether different from ginger ale.

5 oz Jamaican ginger, 2 oz honey, 2 oz lime juice, 1 egg white, 1½ lb sugar, ½ oz fresh or ¼ oz dry yeast, several drops of Angostura bitters.

Pound the ginger. Mix the ginger, sugar, honey, and lime juice with 2 quarts water in a large jug. Dissolve the yeast in a spoonful of water and add with the beaten egg white. Stir to blend. Allow to stand in a cool, dark place. After a few days,

...ndicate the beginnings of fermentation... ...several more days, this should ...ing that the ginger beer is ready. ...ough cheesecloth before serving or ...ing. Sweeten to taste.

...can Shandy It is essential to use Jamaican Ginger Beer with Red Stripe, a very light and quenching Jamaican lager beer. Serves two.

2 cans lager, 1 pint ginger beer.

Stir gently over 2 ice cubes in large stemmed glasses.

Japanese Cocktail This is a recognized recipe, although a more Japanese drink would be an Alexander made with Suntory whiskey and green tea liqueur.

2 oz cognac, 1 teaspoon almond extract or $\frac{1}{4}$ oz orgeat, 1 or more dashes Angostura bitters, 1 teaspoon lime juice (optional), 1 sliver lemon peel.

Shake with cracked ice, and strain into a cocktail glass. Decorate with the lemon peel.

Jockey Club One authority maintains this is a sweet Manhattan with two dashes of maraschino to each drink. The Savoy version is more commonly accepted.

2 oz gin, 2 dashes crème de noyau, 4 dashes lemon juice, orange bitters and Angostura bitters to taste.

Shake thoroughly with ice cubes, and strain into a cocktail glass.

John Collins See **The Collins**

Julep See **Mint Julep**

Kahlúa Java A thoroughly sickly treat. Serves eight.

2 pints hot coffee, 2 pints hot cocoa, 1 oz (or more) Kahlúa, marshmallows.

Stir in a chafing dish, and serve in mugs, each topped with a marshmallow.

Kangaroo The facts are that Australians drink beer, and the spirit historically connected with their homeland is rum, but this vodka cocktail is universally accepted as a Kangaroo. It is a less offensive name than Vodkatini.

1$\frac{1}{2}$ oz vodka, $\frac{3}{4}$ oz dry vermouth, 1 twist lemon peel (optional).

Stir with ice, and serve straight up in a cocktail glass, or on the rocks in an Old Fashioned glass, with a twist of lemon peel.

Kentucky Colonel This name is sometimes given to a mix of bourbon and pineapple juice, although that is surely the unranked version.

1$\frac{1}{2}$ oz bourbon, 2 teaspoons Bénédictine.

Stir with ice, and serve o.
Fashioned glass.

Kerry Cooler Nothing as disgust.
have come from the kingdom of K.

> 2 oz Irish whiskey, 1 oz dry sherry, 1 tab.
> almond extract, 1 tablespoon (or more) lem.
> juice, soda, 1 lemon slice.

Shake well with ice cubes. Serve on the rocks in a
Collins glass, topped up with soda, and decorated
with the lemon slice.

Kingston One widely accepted recipe is for a nasty
mixture of rum, gin, lime or lemon juice and
optional grenadine. The following is bizarre, bu
no less workable.

> 1 oz Jamaica rum, 2 teaspoons kümmel,
> 2 teaspoons orange juice, 1 dash Pimento liqueur.

Shake well with ice cubes, and strain into a cocktail glass.

Kirsch and Cassis A very sweet but typically French
drink for warm afternoons at the pavement café.

> ♥ 2 oz crème de cassis, 1 oz kirsch, soda.

The French just pour and stir, but there is much
to be said for shaking with cracked ice, to cool
thoroughly and slightly dilute. Serve in a *ballon*
wine glass with 2 to 3 ice cubes. Top up with soda.

Kir A very popular and agreeable French apéritif,
named after Canon Kir, heroic wartime mayor
of Dijon, and left-wing politician.

> 1 teaspoon to 2 tablespoons crème de cassis (or
> blackcurrant juice), 4 oz chilled white burgundy.

Pour the wine over the blackcurrant juice in a
ballon wine glass. Ice optional.

Knickerbocker The regular version of this cocktail
is a rather ordinary mixture of gin with two tea-
♥ spoons of dry vermouth and one of sweet vermouth. The Special is a drinker's fruit salad.

> 1 teaspoon raspberry syrup, 1 teaspoon lemon or
> lime juice, 1 teaspoon orange juice, ½ teaspoon
> curaçao (optional), 2 oz light rum. A teaspoon
> of pineapple juice or crushed pineapple and/or a
> slice of pineapple as decoration are optional.

Shake very thoroughly with crushed ice, and
strain into a cocktail glass.

Ladies' Cocktail A quaint name which is evidence
of bartenders' prejudices, but there is nothing
especially gentle about the drink.

> 1½–2 oz bourbon, ½ teaspoon (or more) Pernod,
> ½ teaspoon (or less) anisette, 2 dashes (or more)
> Angostura bitters, pineapple pieces.

Stir with ice cubes, and strain into a cocktail
glass. Decorate with pineapple.

though it

rtini
amaro

bubbling
mentation,
cease, indica
Strain thr
bottling

bian...
(Ita... cherry
Sha... Another v...
glas...nd maraschino.

Leave... or Plymouth gin, ½ oz dr...
ras... apricot brandy, 1 dash grenad...
1 o...
ve... juice.
1 ... ice, and strain into a cocktail glass.
S... can be made drier with less sweet ver-

Libe... and more Picon.
... Canadian whisky, 1½ oz sweet vermouth,
...ashes Amer Picon, a dash of orange bitters.
Shake with ice cubes and serve with ice in an Old Fashioned glass.

Liberty Another version blends 1½ oz of apricot brandy with ½ to 1 oz sloe gin.
1½ oz apple brandy, 1 tablespoon (or more) white rum, a few drops of sugar syrup.
Stir with ice, and strain into a cocktail glass.

Lillet Cocktail This makes use of a delicate vermouth which deserves a bigger reputation. Add a teaspoon of crème de noyau for a yet more interesting apéritif.
1½ oz Lillet, 1 tablespoon dry gin, 1 twist of lemon.
Stir with ice. Serve with the twist of lemon in a cocktail glass or in an Old Fashioned glass.

Limey Liqueurs made from limes are not always easy to find. Spain has one called Crema de Lima.
1 oz light rum, 1½ tablespoons lime liqueur, 2 teaspoons triple sec, 2 teaspoons lime juice, 1 sliver lime.
Mix in a blender at low speed for 15 seconds with 3 oz crushed ice. Strain into a saucer-shaped champagne glass. Decorate with the sliver of lime.

Los Angeles The ingredients are familiar. Just add an egg.
1½ oz bourbon, 1 dash Italian sweet vermouth, 1–1½ teaspoons sugar, 1 egg.
Shake with ice cubes, and strain into a small saucer-shaped champagne glass, or serve on the rocks in an Old Fashioned glass.

Louisiana Lullaby This is appropriately Francophile.
1½ oz dark rum, 2 teaspoons dark Dubonnet, 2 to 3 drops Grand Marnier, 1 sliver lemon.

Stir with ice,
Decorate with the

Madeira Mint Flip A ra
and chocolate mint liq
1½ oz madeira, 1 tablespoo
liqueur, 1½ teaspoons (or less
1 egg, grated nutmeg, grate
Shake very thoroughly with ice, a
a cocktail glass. Decorate with th
grated chocolate.

★**Mai-Tai** The name is similar to that of a m
Chinese liquor, but sweet Mai-Tai
classic cocktail.
1 lime, ½ oz curaçao, ¼ oz rock candy syrup
sugar), ¼ oz orgeat syrup, 2 oz Trader Vic
Tai rum or 1 oz dark Jamaica rum and 1 oz
or medium rum (preferably Martinique), the
peel of 1 lime, pineapple pieces, cocktail
cherries or fresh mint sprigs.
Squeeze the lime juice over shaved ice in an Old
Fashioned or Collins glass. Add the rest of the
ingredients. Decorate with the lime peel, the
pineapple and the cherry, or mint.

Manhattan One of the basic cocktails, usually made
with rye, although some drinkers prefer bourbon.
Bitters, usually Angostura, are essential. Some
drinkers also like to have a drop of orange
bitters. Others prefer a sweetener like maraschino
cherry juice. A regular Manhattan comprises:
1½–2 oz rye, and 1 oz Italian sweet vermouth.
A Dry Manhattan employs only French vermouth; a Perfect has the same amount of vermouth, but half Italian sweet and half French
dry; a Sweet has Italian vermouth only. Like all
classics, the Manhattan inspires great debate as
to exactly which ingredients, and in what proportion, make the true cocktail.
2½ oz rye, 1 oz Italian sweet vermouth.
Stir well with ice cubes, and strain into a cocktail
glass. Decorate with a maraschino cherry, or a
twist of lemon for the Dry.

★**Margarita** A modern classic.
1–2 oz tequila, ½ oz triple sec (preferably
Cointreau), the juice of ½ lime.
Shake very thoroughly with cracked ice, or use a
blender. Strain into a cocktail or saucer-shaped
champagne glass rimmed with salt.

Martini See **Dry Martini**

Mayan Whore From down Mexico way, or just from
southern California? In fact, the recipe comes
from the Jerome Hotel, Aspen, Colorado.

1½ oz tequila, 1 oz Kahlúa, 3 oz chilled pineapple juice, soda.

Pour first the tequila, then the pineapple juice. Top up with soda and then float the Kahlúa on top. Do not stir. Let the drink stand like a layered Pousse-café, and drink through a straw.

Merry Widow Is it the need to drown sorrows, or the imagined availability of the widow, that makes this name so popular among cocktail barmen? There are several variations, all of them standard cocktails. A naked Merry Widow is called a Mary Garden.

1½ oz Dubonnet, 1½ oz dry French vermouth.

Stir well with ice, and strain into a cocktail glass. Add a twist of lemon peel, and the drink is metamorphosed from a Mary Garden into a Merry Widow. Or, instead of the lemon peel, add a dash of orange bitters. An excellent apéritif. A quite different, and much sweeter, Merry Widow is made with 1½ oz cherry brandy and 1½ oz maraschino, shaken.

Serve with ice in a cocktail glass topped with a cherry.

Merry Widow Fizz is the same as Gin Fizz, but half of the lemon juice is replaced by orange juice.

Merry Widower is made with:

1½ oz London Dry gin, 1½ oz dry French vermouth, 2 dashes Pernod, a dash of bitters, and 2 dashes Bénédictine.

Shake, strain over ice, and serve with a twist of lemon peel, in a cocktail glass.

Milk Punches 2–3 oz whisky or brandy of choice, ½ pint milk, 1 teaspoon sugar.

Shake with cracked ice until blended, then strain into a long glass. Dust with nutmeg, and decorate with orange peel. Or, for a most effective nightcap, mix the liquor and sugar, then pour into a mug or a glass with a handle, followed by hot (but not boiling) milk.

White Flush is a milk punch made with gin, and sometimes with maraschino instead of sugar.

Bull's Milk is made with 2 parts rum to 3 parts brandy.

Tiger's Milk is an ambitious drink made with applejack, sugar, ½ an egg white, a hint of vanilla essence, the same of orange essence, a clove and a piece of cinnamon. The egg white is beaten, then shaken with the flavourings, liquor and ice, strained into a long glass, and topped with equal proportions of milk and sweet cider. Clench your stomach, and swallow for dear life.

★Mint Julep Redolent of the South, with pulchritudinous young women lolling provocatively on the porch, or in a swing, waiting for a long drink to cool, or inflame, passions. Different passions are inflamed over the merits of various mixing techniques. As always, it is a matter of taste. Frost a long glass in the refrigerator before you start.

4 mint sprigs, 1 teaspoon or cube of sugar, a swoosh of soda or ½ small cup water, crushed ice, 2–3 oz bourbon.

Take at least a dozen small, tender leaves from 2 of the mint sprigs and muddle them gently with the sugar, in a bar glass. Pour on the bourbon and soda or water, and stir gently until the sugar is completely dissolved. Strain into the frosted glass packed with crushed ice. Stir with a long spoon. Rinse the remaining mint sprigs in cold water, dry them with a clean towel, dip them in powdered sugar, clip the ends of the stems to release juice, and immerse them in the glass as a garnish. Serve with straws. Some barmen add 3 dashes of Angostura to the mixing glass. Some top the drink with a splash of rum. Some argue passionately against any stirring.

★Mojito A rum Collins, with sprigs of mint.

★Monkey Gland Not a steak, but a refreshing short cocktail. A good apéritif if the mix is not too sweet.

1½ oz gin, 1 generous tablespoon fresh orange juice, a generous few drops of Bénédictine, and the same again of grenadine.

Stir with ice in a mixing glass, then strain into an Old Fashioned glass, over plenty of ice.

★Montana Perhaps a restorative in the mountain cold, and a marvellous antidote for sickly stomachs or weak knees.

2 oz brandy, 2 teaspoons port, 2 teaspoons dry vermouth.

Stir, and serve with one cube of ice in a cocktail glass.

★Moscow Mule An American invention, of course. A very refreshing long cocktail, and you can vary the amount of vodka to adjust the kick of the mule.

2–3 oz vodka, the juice of ½ lime, 1 twist lime peel, ginger beer (preferably ginger ale), cucumber peel.

Add 2 ice cubes, stir and serve in a Collins glass. Garnish with the cucumber peel.

Mount Fuji An explosive standard cocktail, but this spectacular version is from the Beverly Hilton.

1½ oz light rum, 1½ oz applejack, 1 oz Southern Comfort, 1 oz sugar, the juice of ½ lime, crushed ice. For the flambéed finale, 1 oz of 75% (151 US proof) rum, and the scooped-out shell of the ½ lime.

Combine the ingredients in a blender to produce an icy, alcoholic lava, and empty this into a Sour glass, or something more elaborate, to make a mountain. Place the scooped-out lime shell on top, inverted like a crater, fill with the explosive rum, ignite and admire the volcanic scene. As the heat melts the icy lava, drink with a straw.

Mulled Wine Fun for a party, and almost obligatory after skiing. Serves about six.

2 bottles red wine, ¼ bottle port, ¼ bottle brandy, the peel of 1 orange and 1 lemon, grated nutmeg, 6 cloves, 1 or 2 pieces cinnamon, 1 tablespoon brown sugar.

Bring all the ingredients almost to the boil, stirring with a wooden spoon, and simmer for 5 minutes. Serve in mugs.

Negroni An elegant apéritif, with a vaguely Broadway flavour.

2 oz dry gin, 1 oz sweet Italian vermouth, 1 oz Campari, 1 slice orange.

Pour over large cubes of ice in a *ballon* wine glass. Stir well. Add the orange slice.

Old Fashioned A classic whiskey cocktail, for which there are countless recipes. The whiskey must be American, and some argue specifically for rye. Some argue that the sugar should be in the form of syrup; others accept cubes muddled with water. Some hold out for Angostura bitters; others favour Peychaud.

Pour into an Old Fashioned glass 2 teaspoons sugar syrup and add 3 dashes bitters. Stir thoroughly with a spoon. Add 1½ oz rye and stir again. Add 3 large cubes cracked ice. Top up with whiskey and stir again.

Some drinkers like a swoosh of soda; others object. Add a twist of lemon to the drink. Garnish with a slice of orange and, if you must, a maraschino cherry. An Old Fashioned can be agreeably embellished with a dash of curaçao.

Olympia Dark rum is preferred in the classic recipe for this cocktail, but a light rum version is also popular.

1 teaspoon cherry brandy, usually Danish, 1 oz lime juice, 2 oz rum.

Stir well with plenty of ice, and strain into a cocktail glass.

★Olympic A delightfully refreshing cocktail to round
off lunch on a warm summer day.

 *¾ oz brandy, ¾ oz curaçao, ¾ oz (or vary to taste)
fresh orange juice.*

Stir well with plenty of ice, and strain into a
cocktail glass.

One Ireland A Republican ambition, of course, as
can be seen by the colour of the ingredients. Do
not ask for this drink in the wrong part of Belfast.
Otherwise delicious on a rare hot afternoon in
any of the 32 counties.

 *1 oz Irish whiskey, 1 tablespoon crème de menthe,
2 oz vanilla ice-cream.*

Mix thoroughly in a blender. Serve in a cocktail
glass.

Opening A classic cocktail, with interesting flavours,
but rather sweet. Another Opening, another
show?

 *1 oz rye (some barmen prefer Canadian),
2 teaspoons sweet vermouth, 2 teaspoons
grenadine.*

Shake with ice, and serve over plenty of ice in an
Old Fashioned glass. Some barmen prefer to stir.

★Opera A sophisticated cocktail to drink before a
night with the Marx Brothers.

 *1½ oz gin, preferably London Dry, 1 teaspoon (or
more, to taste) Dubonnet, 1 teaspoon
maraschino.*

Optional extras are orange peel, or the tiniest
squeeze of juice. Shake well with ice, and strain
into a cocktail glass. Decorate with orange peel
or a slice of orange.

★Orange Bloom There are at least 20 mixed drinks in
which orange is the dominant flavour, but the
classic variations are the Blossom, the Fizz and
the Bloom.

 *1 oz gin, preferably London Dry, 2 teaspoons
Cointreau, 2 teaspoons Italian sweet vermouth.*

Shake with ice, and strain over ice into a cocktail
glass.

Orange Blossom This is sometimes known as the
Adirondack. Originally, in the Prohibition period, a modest blush of orange was used to
disguise an enormous slug of gin, and there was
nothing more to it. Today, a more civilized version is in order and there are a great many
amusing variations.

 *1½ oz gin, ½ oz orange juice, 2 teaspoons curaçao
(optional), 2 teaspoons fresh lemon or fresh lime
juice, a couple of drops of orange-flower water,
1 teaspoon sugar syrup, 1 orange slice.*

Shake with plenty of ice, or use a blender, in which case an egg white may be added. Strain and serve in a Sour glass with plenty of ice. Add the orange slice.

★*Orange Fizz* A variation on the Gin Fizz.

▮ *2 oz gin, 2 tablespoons lemon juice, 2 teaspoons triple sec, 1½ teaspoons sugar syrup, 2 dashes orange bitters, soda, orange juice, 1 orange slice.*
Shake with ice. Strain into a Sour glass. Add ice and soda, a squeeze of orange, and the orange slice.

★*Paradise* Sometimes mixed with light rum, but more
▼ commonly with gin.
1½ oz (or more) gin, 1 oz orange juice, 1 oz (or less) apricot brandy.
Shake with cracked ice, and strain into a cocktail glass. Decorate with a thin slice of orange.

Park Lane Special From the Park Lane Hotel,
▼ London. With British eccentricity, the aforesaid
♥ hotel is not quite in Park Lane, but nearby in Piccadilly.
2 oz gin, ⅔ oz apricot brandy (liqueur), juice of ½ fresh orange, dash of grenadine, ½ egg white.
Shake with ice, and strain into a cocktail glass.

Peach West Indies Add crème de banane if you want to change the flavour.
1½ oz light rum, ½ peach, 2 to 3 drops Rose's lime juice, 2 to 3 drops maraschino.
Peel the peach, and combine with the other ingredients and 3 oz crushed ice in a blender at high speed for 15 seconds. Strain into a small saucer-shaped champagne glass.

Peppermint Park Bright young things and ardent
▮ Americanophiles flock to Peppermint Park in London to feed off pastrami on rye (bread, not whiskey), and dig into dazzling cocktails.
2 oz gin, 1 oz sweetened lemon juice, champagne.
Shake the gin and juice thoroughly with ice cubes, and strain into a large champagne saucer. Top up with champagne, and serve with straws.

Picon See *Amer Picon*

Pimm's The invention of James Pimm who ran a
▮ restaurant in London in the 1880s. Pimm devised a gin sling which was so peculiar that he put it into commercial production. His celebrated product, gin flavoured with herbs and liqueurs, anticipated the packaged cocktail by nearly a hundred years. Pimms No 2 (whisky based), No 3 (brandy), No 4 (rum) and No 5 (rye) are no longer produced, but No 6 (vodka) is still available. Although it features in a variety of confec-

tions, Pimm's is a mixed drink in itself, and merely needs serving properly:

3 oz Pimm's No 1, 1 twist cucumber peel, 1 slice lemon, a few borage leaves, plenty of ice, fizzy lemonade or 7-Up. Optional: 1 oz London Dry or Plymouth gin, 1 teaspoon Cointreau.

Serve in a 1-pint glass mug.

★**Piña Colada** Among the mixed drinks which have established themselves in the 1970s, surely none has won such widespread popularity as the Piña Colada.

2–3 oz golden rum, 3–4 oz crushed pineapple, or pineapple juice, 1½–2 oz cream of coconut, pineapple pieces.

Shake, or mix in a blender, with 1 scoop of shaved ice. Pour over more ice in a Collins glass, and serve with a straw. Decorate with the pineapple pieces.

Pink Gin The lingering flavour of smart London— Park Lane, Berkeley Square, and the watering holes of Mayfair between the wars and in the 1940s—although this "sophisticated" drink originated as a medicinal potion in the British navy.

1½ oz Plymouth gin, several drops Angostura bitters.

Shake the bitters into a wine or Martini glass, roll them around, and shake out. Pour in the gin. Ice optional.

★*Pisco Punch* A rare opportunity to use the Pisco brandy of Peru.

3 oz Pisco brandy, 1½ teaspoons sugar syrup, 1 teaspoon lime juice, 1 egg white, Angostura bitters.

Shake with ice cubes, strain into a Sour glass, and add the bitters.

★*Planter's Punch* Made with Myers rum, from Jamaica. A classic mixed drink, though recipes vary.

1½ oz (or more) Jamaica rum, juice of ½ lemon or lime, 3 oz orange juice (optional), 1 teaspoon sugar, soda, 1 slice orange.

Shake well with crushed ice, and pour into a Collins glass. Top up the glass with more ice and a squirt of soda. Churn with a bar spoon. Decorate with the orange slice.

★*Pousse-café* Strictly "our next trick is impossible", according to John Doxat. A Pousse-café is a series of liqueurs in different colours floating on top of each other in the glass. Very sickly, but spectacular if it can be done. Keep the glass very still, and pour the liqueurs over a spoon.

Different liqueurs have different weights, and they must be poured in ascending order of lightness. David Embury suggests the following order: *1. grenadine 2. brown crème de cacao 3. maraschino 4. orange curaçao 5. green crème de menthe 6. parfait amour 7. cognac.*

Use a straight-sided Pousse-café glass, of course.

President See *El Presidente*

Pussyfoot A non-alcoholic cocktail, for an abstaining guest who does not wish to be conspicuous. Several of these drinks were created during the Prohibition era. One modern Pussyfoot has gone back on the bottle, with rum.

1 oz lemon juice, 2 oz orange juice, 1 teaspoon grenadine, ½ egg yolk, 1 cherry.

Shake thoroughly with cracked ice, and pour into a wine glass with 1 or 2 ice cubes. Decorate with the cherry.

Quebec Say Noilly Prat, and your Canadian is perfect.

1½ oz Canadian whisky, 2 teaspoons Noilly Prat dry vermouth, 1 teaspoon Amer Picon, 1 teaspoon maraschino.

Stir with ice in a mixing glass, and serve in a cocktail glass, or an Old Fashioned glass.

Ramos Fizz The morning-after drink before Sunday brunch. A New Orleans Gin Fizz with orange-flower water. Minor variations abound. This recipe comes from Victor, of Ginsberg's Dublin Pub, at Mason and Bay, San Francisco. (Oy Vay, Mason and Bay).

1½ oz gin, ¼ cup half-and-half milk and double cream, 1 egg white, juice of ½ large lemon, 1 heaped teaspoon sugar, 1 teaspoon orange-flower water.

Shake with crushed ice, and strain into a Highball glass.

The Rickey A medium-sized drink usually flavoured with lime, most commonly based on gin, and made to a fairly dry mix. Invented by a "Colonel" Rickey, from Kentucky.

2 oz dry gin, 1 oz fresh lime juice (lemon is the alternative), 1 or more dashes grenadine, 1 long twist lime peel, soda.

Mix the ingredients with 1 cube of ice in an Old Fashioned glass. Immerse a substantial twist of peel. Top up with soda, and stir very thoroughly with a bar spoon.

Rose of Warsaw A recipe from Paris.

1½ oz Wyborowa Polish vodka, 1 oz Wisniak cherry liqueur, ½ oz Cointreau, 1 dash Angostura.

Stir with ice in a mixing glass, and serve in a cocktail glass.

Road Runner From Al Arteaga, Cathedral Canyon
♈ Country Club, Palm Springs.
♥ *1 oz vodka, ½ oz Amaretto, ½ oz coconut juice, nutmeg.*
Shake thoroughly with cracked ice, and strain into a cocktail glass. Sprinkle with nutmeg.

★**Rusty Nail** Some suggest that the ingredients should
♈ be matched 1:1. Even 2:1 produces too sticky a drink.
1½ oz scotch whisky, 1 oz Drambuie.
Serve in a cocktail glass without ice, floating the Drambuie on top, or in an Old Fashioned glass with a couple of ice cubes. Do not stir, not even with a rusty nail.

Sangaree Originally a sweetened fortified wine
▮ served in a tumbler, and often iced. An old Anglicization of the Spanish word Sangria. This is the Savoy Sangaree.
1 teaspoonful powdered sugar, 1 large glass sherry or port, 1 slice orange or 1 twist lemon peel, nutmeg.
Stir well, and strain into an Old Fashioned glass. Add the orange slice or lemon peel, and dust with nutmeg.

★**Sangria** An essential part of a holiday in Spain.
▮ Serves four.
1 bottle Spanish dry red wine, 2 oz Spanish brandy, 1 oz curaçao or similar liqueur, 3 oz lemon juice, 3 oz orange juice, 2 oz sugar, ½ orange, sliced.
Stir ingredients in a jug, and serve in large wine glasses.

★**Sazerac** A New Orleans drink. Lots of ritual empha-
♈ sized by David Embury, and a heavy rye demanded by Trader Vic.
2 oz rye, 1 teaspoon sugar syrup, a few drops of Pernod, 1 to 3 dashes Peychaud bitters, 1 twist lemon peel.
Stir the rye, sugar and bitters in a mixing glass with ice until they are thoroughly chilled. Chill an Old Fashioned glass with crushed ice, then discard the ice. Rinse the glass with Pernod, and empty it. Strain the whiskey into the glass. Twist the lemon peel over the glass. The peel can then be immersed in the drink, or used to decorate an accompanying glass which has been filled with iced water as a chaser.

The Scaffa An old term, the meaning of which is no
134 ♈ longer clear. It is generally agreed to mean a

drink in which a spirit and a liqueur share a small glass with a dash or two of bitters, but there is doubt over a Pousse-café dimension. Brandy, maraschino, and perhaps green Chartreuse, are candidates for inclusion.

Screwdriver Supposedly invented by oilmen who stirred it with their screwdrivers.

1½ oz vodka, orange juice to taste.

Pour the vodka into an Old Fashioned or Collins glass, with plenty of ice, and add the juice. Stir.

Shamrock Variation on *Everybody's Irish*, with vermouth.

Shirley Temple A kids' cocktail.

A dash of grenadine in a large champagne glass full of 7-Up or ginger ale, decorated with cherries. No alcohol.

The Shrub A drink which is made by soaking fruit or peel, traditionally lemons, in liquor, with sugar. An old English idea. The Shrub is kept for not less than a week, and preferably five or six weeks, before being used. The liquor may then be drunk straight, or diluted. Serves two dozen.

2 quarts Jamaica rum or brandy, 1 pint (or less) lemon juice, grated rind of 2 to 3 lemons, 2 lb sugar.

Soak the lemon rind in the rum for 2 to 3 days. Add the sugar to 1 quart water, and heat until it has dissolved. Mix all the ingredients, strain and bottle. Seal the bottle tightly, and store in a cool place. Serve in brandy snifter, with a slice of orange.

Sidecar The drinker who invented this cocktail used to travel by sidecar to the Paris bistro which originally made it for him during the First World War. The drink was popularized by Harry's Bar in Paris.

2 oz cognac or armagnac, ½ oz lemon juice, ¼ oz Cointreau, 1 twist lemon peel.

Shake thoroughly with plenty of cracked ice, and strain into a cocktail glass. Decorate with the lemon peel.

Silk Stockings A very sickly recipe from Mexico.

1½ oz white tequila, 2 oz evaporated milk, 1 oz crème de cacao, 1 oz grenadine, ground cinnamon, 1 cherry.

Mix with cracked ice in a blender. Strain into a cocktail glass. Sprinkle with cinnamon, and decorate with the cherry.

The Sling A sweetish long drink, traditionally based on gin, often containing cherry brandy, and sometimes topped with water rather than soda.

135

The basic Gin Sling of *The Savoy Cocktail Book* contains only the spirit, sugar, water and one lump of ice. The Singapore Sling, from Raffles Hotel, also contains cherry brandy.

2oz gin, 1oz cherry brandy, 1oz lemon juice, soda (optional).

Shake well, and strain into a Highball or Collins glass, with 1 ice cube. Top up with water or soda.

The Smash A shorter **Mint Julep**, usually served in ♈ an Old Fashioned glass, and often made with brandy.

The Sour The most basic of the several classic mixed-🔖 drink categories which comprise spirit, citrus and sugar. It should be sour, and it may be served without any ice or other trimmings in its own stemmed glass, rather like an overgrown apéritif cocktail. The original is the Whiskey Sour.

2oz bourbon or rye, ½oz lemon juice, ¼oz sugar syrup.

Shake well with ice cubes, and strain into a Sour glass.

Spritzer A hock-and-seltzer—a mixture which is 🔖 rarely demanded, but wonderfully refreshing.

3oz chilled dry white Rhine wine, 2oz soda or Apollinaris water.

Pour the wine first, into a large *ballon* wine glass. Top up with soda or Apollinaris water to two-thirds full. Do not ice.

★ **The Stinger** A 1½oz jigger of any spirit (name your ♈ poison), and 1oz white crème de menthe or peppermint schnapps.

Shake with cracked ice, and strain into a cocktail glass, or serve on the rocks in an Old Fashioned glass. Brandy is best.

Strega Flip The distinctive Italian liqueur is also ♈ used to flavour a gin-based Strega Sour.

1oz Strega, 1oz brandy, 2 teaspoons orange juice, 1½ teaspoons sugar syrup, 1 teaspoon lemon juice, 1 egg, nutmeg.

Shake very thoroughly with cracked ice, and strain into a cocktail glass. Dust with nutmeg.

Tennessee Jack Daniel's might be preferred.

♈ *3oz rye, 2 tablespoons maraschino, 2 teaspoons lemon juice.*

Shake with ice cubes, and serve on the rocks in an Old Fashioned glass.

★ **Tequila Sunrise** The ingredients are poured straight 🔖 into the glass, with the grenadine providing the sunrise, but there is disagreement as to which order of elements achieves this best. A Tequila Sunset is made with golden tequila, lemon juice and light honey. A Tijuana Sunrise has Angostura bitters instead of grenadine.

¾oz grenadine, 1½oz tequila, 4oz orange juice.
Usually served on the rocks in an Old Fashioned glass, although the effect can be better in a large cocktail glass, straight up.

hanksgiving Cocktail To build an appetite for the ♈ turkey in November.

1oz dry gin, 1oz dry vermouth, 1oz apricot brandy, a few drops lemon juice, 1 cherry.
Shake with ice cubes, and strain into a cocktail glass. Decorate with the cherry.

Tom Collins See **Collins**

Union Jack The gin may be English, but the violet-♈ petal liqueur was named after the French actress Yvette Gilbert.

1½oz London Dry gin, 1 tablespoon Crème Yvette.
Shake well with crushed ice, and strain into a cocktail glass.

Via Veneto Sambuca Romana must be the preferred ♈ brand.

1¾oz Italian brandy, 2 teaspoons sambuca, 2 teaspoons lemon juice, 1½ teaspoons sugar syrup, ½ egg white.
Shake well with crushed ice, and strain into a cocktail glass.

Whiskey Sour See **The Sour**

White Satin A recipe from The Netherlands.
♈ *1oz Galliano, 1oz Tia Maria, 1oz double cream.*
♥ Shake well with crushed ice, and strain into a cocktail glass.

Xeres A corruption of Jerez? Surprisingly, it's not.
♈ *3oz dry sherry, 1 to 2 dashes orange bitters, 1 to 2 dashes peach bitters.*
Shake well with ice cubes, and strain into a cocktail glass.

Zombie "A joke drink," say the bartenders of ♟ Britain, through their professional guild. No doubt their counterparts elsewhere in the world agree. The object is to get as many different rums as possible into one drink, like students in a telephone box.

1½oz golden rum, 1 tablespoon Jamaica rum, 1 tablespoon light rum, 3 tablespoons lime juice, 1 tablespoon pineapple and 1 tablespoon papaya or passion-fruit juice, 1½ teaspoons sugar syrup.
Shake, or mix in a blender, with a scoop of shaved ice. Serve over more ice in a tall glass. Float a teaspoon of 151-proof rum on top, and sprinkle with sugar. Decorate with elaborate garnishes.

The hangover—how to cure it

Considering the misery which it causes, the hangover has yielded disappointingly little to serious medical research, but the following remedies do have at least some scientific basis.

1. If you can think about measures beforehand without spoiling your evening, then the precautionary glass of milk really is worth while. It will retard the absorption of alcohol, and protect your stomach against the worst consequent irritations.

2. If you are prepared to be bored, drink only vodka or one of the other relatively pure continuous-still spirits. The more individualistic pot-still spirits, like brandies and malt whiskies, are more likely to contain traces of toxic higher alcohols. Since no two whiskies or brandies are alike, it is worth experimenting to find one that doesn't hurt.

3. Some vermouths and digestifs may contain tiny traces of toxic compounds deriving from their plant content, though this is open to argument. The same is held to be true of fortified wines, and to a lesser extent of ordinary wines and beers. Only the latter are likely to be drunk in quantity, but it is worth watching out for labels that bring headaches.

4. Alcohol causes dehydration because it is a diuretic. So is coffee, which may therefore make you feel worse. Drink water before you go to bed, and leave some handy in case you wake up in the night. Dehydration also causes that trembly feeling.

5. An irritated stomach may produce acid. That is why antacid patent medicines can be helpful (though caution is advised if they contain aspirin). Mineral waters are alkaline as well as being quenching, so they are doubly useful. Chilled Perrier is excellent, and Kingsley Amis recommends Vichy.

6. Sleep helps the body recover. For the same reason, a tired or unfit drinker is especially vulnerable to hangovers—and no two people respond in quite the same way to each different drink.

7. A bath is refreshing, and cleanses the soul.

8. Vitamin C helps the liver detoxify the blood, and B vitamins may be beneficial.

9. Fructose helps the body metabolize alcohol. It also replaces blood sugar, which may be low in the morning. A low level of blood sugar makes you feel weak. Eat bread and honey.

10. Jewish remedy: to combat dehydration, upset stomach and hunger, drink chicken soup.

Hair of the dog: this replaces lost blood sugar, but sets you on the way to another hangover.